What You Hear in the Dark

SONIA GERNES

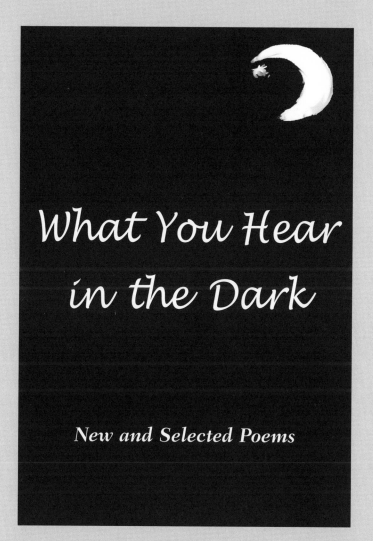

What You Hear in the Dark

New and Selected Poems

UNIVERSITY OF NOTRE DAME PRESS
NOTRE DAME, INDIANA

Copyright © 2006 by Sonia Gernes

Published by the University of Notre Dame Press

Notre Dame, Indiana 46556

www.undpress.nd.edu

All Rights Reserved

Manufactured in the United States of America

Library of Congress Cataloging-in-Publication Data

Gernes, Sonia.

What you hear in the dark : new and selected poems / Sonia Gernes.

p.   cm.

ISBN-13: 978-0-268-02968-5 (pbk. : alk. paper)

ISBN-10: 0-268-02968-7 (pbk. : alk. paper)

I. Title.

PS3557.E685W44   2006

811'.54—dc22

2006001547

∞ The paper in this book meets the guidelines for permanence and durability
of the Committee on Production Guidelines for Book Longevity of the Council on
Library Resources.

for friends and family, sources of light —

Contents

from   *A Breeze Called the Fremantle Doctor* (1997)

Selections from The Indian School

Selections from
A BREEZE CALLED THE FREMANTLE DOCTOR

Acknowledgments

Grateful acknowledgment is made to the editors of the following publications where these poems first appeared:

Georgia Review:
"Jazz"

Hopewell Review:
"The Bank," "Traps," "Rings," "Sight Is a Species of Touch"

Indiana Review:
"The First Year of Living Alone," "The Glazier's Daughter"

I've Always Meant to Tell You, Constance Warloe, ed. (Pocket Books, 1997): "Unnaming the Flowers"

New Letters:
"Poem in Wartime," "Ladyslipper," "The Church Burning," "Geographer"

Poetry Northwest:
"A Table, a Chair, a Yellow Balloon"

Seattle Review:
"Alzheimer's: the Early Years"

I am indebted to many for support and feedback in writing these poems. They include: Carole Walton, Joan McIntosh, Max Westler, Jessica Maich, Julie Herrick White, Jan Seabaugh, Mary Gerhart, Carole Glickfeld; my colleagues in the Creative Writing Program at the University of Notre Dame: Valerie Sayers, William O'Rourke, John Matthias, Orlando Menes, Kymberly Taylor, Steve Tomasula, and Matthew Benedict; and my editor, Katie Lehman.

Some of these poems were written under a Creative Writing Fellowship from the National Endowment for the Arts which made possible their creation.

NEW POEMS

I. Unnaming the Flowers

Flyboys

The young uncles released us from time,
flying west to east in a tiny plane
they rented jointly, landing
wind-socked and grinning on a ribbon
of pasture our town called a landing strip.

World War II taught them time zones
and bold women—Italy, the Philippines,
Francis and the floozy named Kaye—
big boobs, big voice, stockings-in-a-bottle
painting a dark seam down the back of her legs.

G.I. Bill lessons put them back in the sky,
solo and climbing, every atom intact,
time becoming distance—the tines
of a pitchfork circling a compass point—
the future a yonder still blue, still wild.

2.

They settled down to farms and movie cameras:
"Act natural, now," as we goaded
our bikes down the crushed rock drive,
leaped on and off the tractor seat,
watched our mother emerge

from the chicken coop, scowling slightly
at her pail of eggs, then laughing
abashed, a hand up to shade herself,
girlish in the glare of the unrehearsed.
Next, the projector, the ironed sheet.

We liked ourselves best in reverse.
"See Sophie back into the chicken coop,"
an uncle would say. "See Norbert
back-pedal up the hill." And there
we would be: plucking popcorn

out of our mouths, whole and dry,
handfuls tumbling from my brother's
greedy lips, the banana in my hand
building bite by bit, my fingers inspired,
the magic peel zipped.

3.

What was it that we loved—causality
reversed? Time leaping its linear track?
Our own moment in Einstein's inertial frame—
a present we could eternally rehearse?
Or was it some hope, some comfort, that tossed

in time's accelerant, we would not be flame
and loss—that some shape, flickering and slight,
could slide through space—that even among
inconstant stars, our world revolves eastward,
darkness ever spinning toward the light?

Sight Is a Species of Touch

It's what my father said,
guiding me past the yardlight's reach
the autumn I turned nine—
the autumn I watched my mother swell,
the fetus dying within her
and nowhere to go but on.

"See with your feet," my father said
and turned off his flash.
"Ditches are slicker than the gravel bed,
culverts can trick you, but feel the little rise,
and don't count on the moon—
there's danger in its cycles."

Where were we going
that moonless night?
Neighbors? The white frame schoolhouse
where farmers ate thick sandwiches,
played *Schafskopf*, and called it PTA?

That part is gone,
but not the whispered rasp
of corn I could not see,
not the murmurs
of slight, noctural beasts
in the fields' cold womb

not the darkness
when my father let go my hand
and I stepped, stepped
knowing he could not take me
the distance I'd need to go,
could not even light
the longing that propelled me
into dark and luring air.

The Houses of Ill Repute

The houses of ill repute
were stitched along the tracks
on Second Street, the clumsy seam
of river, town, and blood-brick depot
that crumbled at our feet.

It was the early Fifties;
train service was already slowing down,
when my mother propelled me
in a burst of steam
past houses whose very wickedness
was a centripetal force
mothers with daughters
must brace against.

"Ill repute,"
was all the explanation she would give,
and for years I conjured those houses' offense:
       eaves that whispered
       obscenely in the wind,
       guilty doors,
       cellars caressing their own warm damp,
       the smell of sin.

But that was not where she lost me.
In secret, I joined those floorboards to sound,
syllables to sense, amorphous desire
to the flat sheet-rock of the page—
fingering my own habit of words,
a habit of conjoining so intense
it would suck a daughter down
more deeply than anything carnal.

The Bank

Our only museum wasn't one,
but a flight of marble stairs
above the tellers, above the vault,
where my mother took me
up, up in my feed-sack dress,
past the leopard, the dik dik, the ears
of an elephant shot in 1924
by Mr. & Mrs. E. L. King,
owners of the bank, the factory,
the three-ton hippo, the paychecks
of nearly half the town.

"Anyone can look," my mother said,
though we had no account,
no target of wealth
in the rooms of guns, of spears, the cases
of klipspringer, waterbuck, wildebeast,
horns like an ice tongs clamping down.

"Safari," my mother said. "Africa.
Ten thousand dollars to sleep in a tent!"
and I knew then
that our lives were small,
our journeys constrained, our fate
written somewhere outside these walls
where Mr. & Mrs. E. L. King
financed the jeep, the guides,
the warthog's smirking snout,
the immunity their trophies claimed
against that fast, hard shaft
into the one country
all of us will enter.

Ladyslipper

Forbidden orchid, little womb, blushing in last year's undigested leaves, you were what we craved—lone children, even together in our fathers' woods, spring come at last and we (puddle-drunk as cummings would say) sloshing our way through vernal ravines where newness exploded around our boots: hepatica, blood-root, yellow violet, Indian pipes with their skeletal white, more fungus than flower, but fecund still—a world of vegetable sex we wandered through with what we did not know was innocence, and everything ours—the blossoms, the moss, the geode cracked open (a womb of spiky crystalline), even the softening tar of the flume that descended like a chute, channeling runoff from the fields. Only one *shalt not*. One flower it was larceny to pluck—official flower of our state, fairest of them all, pink slipper sized to the grimy Cinderella of our thumbs—one flower already half extinct, as houses seeped out from towns and sprouted in the once-wild valleys.

We understood. We did not understand. Bluff children, forest roamers, combing the ravines past slopes where sheep and cattle grazed, we knew the bolder face of danger—the neighbor's bull strafing the air behind his fence, the stranger with a car door open—but left on our own to enter a place where nature went its way without thought or guilt or any sense it ought to control itself (*Bless me, Father*), we sensed the danger of the incipient, the unspoken, the thing withheld, the terrain, pink with desire, of one fleshy slipper, one perfect little sac, one knowledge it would take us many springs to gain: there is life, and there is longing, and in our species, one does not cease before the other.

Golden

for my parents' fiftieth anniversary

In the old photographs, it is always autumn.
Colors fade to the sepia of remembered thought:
my mother in a flapper dress, my father
proud beside the Model A. They glow
in the light of dreams that I can never know.

What did they think of that autumn
they climbed into the photograph of bride & groom?
That love would conquer?—the Depression yield
more than its tart and scanty fruit?
In a season of scarceness, the bitter root

of her father's death fresh within the house,
they strode from the church believing
in sunlight—the prairie ringing for them,
the October trees all aflame with praise.
Good farmers, they knew how to raise

the future, a steady hand on each day's plow,
patience in the fallow fields, a table
big enough for all who'd need it, hope
in the seedlings, beauty's grace, a faith
that is the opposite of winter's death.

This autumn, I would take the color
of that triumph, the bright praise of trees,
the harvest secure in the heart's high bins;
I would make of them a portrait fit to hold
through time: these trees, these lives, this gold.

Traps

The last time I drove back
and didn't call it home,
I carried boxes up the stairs
behind her, lifted the bone

sheen of her wedding dress
from the blanket chest, awash
in mellowed silk. She puts
it back, says there's no rush

to pack things. But on the floor:
his boots, his milking vest, the old
hat he wore before the stroke.
Both of us know the farm will be sold.

She pulls a fan from a shelf
(two birds in painted flight),
wool socks, a pocket watch
on a shoestring fob, a rifle

stock. "He wasn't like that,"
she says. "He never shot a thing."
"When he was young," she says,
"when the others went hunting,

he'd look for traps in the woods
and spring them with a stick."
She is folding a quilt, but absently;
she is listening for a distant click.

Geographer

for my father, July 1, 1995

Old geographer, your turn has come.
Once before, you ascended—an aeroplane
that "rode dandy" in the fall of '29.
Then life kept you grounded: a wife, a farm,
hailstones and children, the bottom
dropping out of the price of grain.

Evenings, you sat under the lamp
when the milking was done, maps
in your lap, and pages turned
to mountain heights, inland seas,
prevailing winds that never blew
you far from home. You knew
the population of Seattle
when I moved there, dog-earred
the plains of Indiana, the islands
of the far antipodes.

Your own migrations
slid you into silence, a mute
appraisal of choices and daughters
who fling themselves too far,
a stubborn calm that kept me guessing,
that never let you articulate
what it was you thought I'd lost.

Now, the phone rings,
and this time they have not patched
your rickety heart, have not bolted
body to breath, as you pieced
the hayrack, the planters,
spring upon spring.

This I know of a father's death:
sometime in the night an atlas closes;
towns remain, but the routes are gone.
A blunt official slams the station window,
cancels the ticket of all that's left unsaid—
all those soul-torn places
you never took me, father, all
those borders we never crossed.

Alzheimer's: The Early Years

She tells it at breakfast with the grandchildren present:
how none of our dogs died a natural death:
the collie-mix spun out like gravel from the wheels
he chased, the bitch too dumb to dodge the reaper chain,
the sheep-killing hound who couldn't be muzzled,
Rex, Queenie, Shep—a mongrel litany of the years.

Her voice rains on and on, though I try to muzzle
these words, these tales served up like gory presents
in the midst of sweet rolls, ham, a waxed red wheel
of gouda cheese. *Ma, Ma—these kids are years
too young,* I want to say—this whole chain
of thought too bloody, stark, too heedless of death

for city kids on holiday. I steer her toward the present,
but she jumps up again to grab the coffee pot, wheels
into another round: "That one called Fad got shot to death.
Worthless as sin, a cattle-chaser, his muzzle
tracking every neighbor's dog in heat! Five years
of that was plenty. We had my brother get the chain

and take him to the woods." The children muzzle
their astonishment. I see in their eyes wheels
turning wheels. I want to tell them eighty years
can blunt discretion, unlink the cell-based chain
that keeps the mind intact, that she's smelled death
in Grandpa's strokes, must move now to his present

home, a hospice far from farmland, unchaining
sixty years from this land's yoke. "It snowed that year
Fad died," she says. "The neighbor on his Big Wheels
came to say *his* dog was gone. He'd seen them muzzling
together, so we sent him to the woods." Like death's
own bride, his bitch stood guard on Fad's ravine, present

in spite of snow, the lack of food, three days of death-
like silence. "Grandma, that's so sad," a grandchild wheels
about, extends her hand, but the comfort she presents
cannot change the calendar. As we listen, this year's
snow is filling the ravine, is icing the future into a chain
so taut, a web of days so deeply mute and muzzled

my mother's words chain-stitch an emblem for these years:
walk to death the way no cur would walk, no coward wheel:
face forward, eyes present, straight into the muzzle.

A Chair, a Table, a Yellow Balloon

for my mother

Three things to remember,
the doctor says—a test,
a simple memory check, a warding-off
of tiny hammers that harden in the brain,
swell as knuckles do (*Does this hurt?*)
or water on the knee.

Three things, he says
as though she might forget,
and she lines them up
or almost does, but the stethoscope
is cold upon her back, and she breathes,
breathes, at his command,
the light lying down across the wall,
the table stretching to her own white bed
where fingers warmer than these
once found her skin
firm and fair and quick.

Three things? A bed, a lamp, a silky gown . . .
but she reads error in his eyes and starts again:
a yellow flower, she is sure of that,
but as she looks for confirmation
something around her breaks and lifts:
a petal, a yellow sphere,
an oval wordless as the sun.
She hears the doctor's voice,
but the afternoon is a vast white room
where something drifts,
and as he waits, she reaches,
reaches, but cannot catch the string.

Unnaming the Flowers

My mother at the window of her room
stirs the leaves of cyclamen,
the ratty fern, as though some veiny braille
could tell her genus, species, names
that like the names of all her kin,
disperse on airborn wings,
are subject to the wind.

"That plant I had," she says, "that place
we lived . . ." And as her fingers trace
the serrate reniforms, I say the names:
delphinium, a bleeding heart,
monkshood with its poison leaves,
the woody nightshade we called bittersweet,
anemones, the bridal wreath.

But nothing clicks, no label stops
her brain's black rose from blotting out
its name, its class, its journeys through
evolutionary time to this pale room
with metal bed, call-button pull,
the quilt she finished on the farm,
the photos she's turned upside down.

"You," she says, not "Sonia,"
daughter, progeny . . . Her hands
dodder on the marble sill,
move back toward nameless meadows,
nameless brooks, the sun on mountains
newly made, a hill where nothing sees
the petals unwrap, no one stoops
to give a flower its name; nothing is expected
to remember its fruit.

II. What You Hear in the Dark

What You Hear in the Dark

What you hear in the dark
is what you have not become,
the buzz of discontent
that drills small fissures
in the day's attention, the green
longing that sighs through the grass,
moving with small creatures
across the ivy of the hill.

Some nights
you stand at the window
as if the dark could name you,
and some nights
when you read alone by lamplight,
a ticking at the French doors
causes you to turn.
It's the raccoon, hungry for birdseed—
it's a typewriter tapping—
the old Smith Corona you ordered from Sears,
your down-payment on the distance
words were going to take you,
letter by yearning letter
limned so clearly
you would no longer be alone
in the unexpressed, no longer wake
suddenly, for no reason,
listening for sirens, for singing, for trains
so far away they seem a trackless thrum

and God a fierce absence
you must now embrace
or make a lover
of a night so silent
even the universe
ceases to hum.

Headache

Headache, and the marrow grows
behind my eyes, a calabash,
all pulp and pith, no patterned rind,
no connections, no help for the atavistic urge
to drop dazed beside the water hole,
breast to boggy earth-breast, the grass
a murmur of concealment, the brain
a savannah of fog, too depleted
to hope some ganglion, some single
hairy filament perhaps, will ferry
the twitch from footpad to synapse
from air disturbed by the pelican's swoop
to nerves in the spinal column
that will signal *tense! spring!*
and I will hold in my cortex
a captured thought.

ii.

That first migraine when I was twelve—
a genuine pubescent Fourth of July:
scattered black holes, zaps
of comic-book light, a steel bolt
boring from one temple to the next,
and then the throwing-up. Sure
that blindness was on its way,
a tumor bitter as my aunt's,
I fingered the patterns in my quilt,
tried to find a shape for fear, vowed
I'd wear bangs to conceal the scar,

would learn to read Braille lickety-split,
would never wear housedresses or
maroon felt slippers all day long,
blue-veined ankles crossed like swords
above the feeble rayon pom-poms.

iii.

In China,
where bodies were not cut,
cadavers never dissected,
doctors learned through their finger tips.
In Hong Kong, in a temple clinic,
I saw the charts—heads in numbered sections,
hands mapped like air-traffic control. I
was alone; I was not quite desperate;
I flew on to London and three days
of pain in a room with filthy curtains
just off Gloucester Road. I thought
of what I'd already tried: needles
deep in my neck, my spine adjusted,
a pharmacopoeia of drugs and herbs,
my chakras opened. I dreamed
of the clinic of blind doctors
somewhere in Beijing. Reading the body—
the lumps, the bumps, the layers
of skin, they can push things back:
discs, jaws, collarbones, the dislocated
memory that throbs throughout your sleep.
I have presented myself to psychologists too;
my body is still untranslated.

Rings

Once, on Fiji,
I entered a frog named Margaret Thatcher
in a celebrated jumping match
on a night of very little moon.
I wore a lei; she wore
a tiny #4, hopping out brightly
from a cardboard starting gate
in the center of a circled floor.

In my life thus far,
there've been rings within rings,
boredom, sorrow, a decade down the drain,
but that night on Fiji
I knelt at the edge of a painted orb,
crooned: *Come to Mama, Maggie,*
and waved her on with Aussie champagne.

The amazing thing is this:
she came and she came.
With leaps like the faith
we keep hearing about,
she hurled toward my knees,
victory itself, a fate
I could own,
a memory I could catch and tame
for nights like this
when the moon is down.

The Woman Who Spoke in Numbers

a pantoum for Mary Reed

She looks up and says, "Two, three, six,"
this woman whose artery exploded,
blood spiking her brain like pick-up-stix.
"Twelve, seven," she says, a gun reloaded—

this woman whose artery exploded.
"How are you?" I say. "Sorry I'm late."
"Twelve, seven," she says, a gun reloaded
with sorrows she can't calculate.

"How are you?" I say, "Sorry I'm late . . ."
"Five! Four!" Does my lateness combine
with sorrows she tries to calculate?
How much sadness adds up to nine?

Five? Four? Does my lateness combine
the niggling fears I can't articulate?
How much sadness adds up to nine?
How many fissures round out the slate?

The niggling fears I can't articulate?
Blood spiking her brain like pick-up-stix?
How many fissures round out the slate?
She looks up and says, "Two, three, six . . ."

The Birds in Home Depot

A quick *zzzzt* among white rafters.
A stutter of florescence at the corner
of the eye. A thing too small
to bother with, the stock-boy tells me,
too hard to catch among the toilet bowls,
the molding, power sanders
for smoothing over things,
the Dremel with its edge.

Do they mate here—
I want to ask—build
nests of pink fiberglass? Lay
tiny eggs on the purest of sea sponges,
huddle in the palm of a roofer's glove?
What winged promise lured them in,
so out of nature in these slung
metal branches, these soffets of vacancy?

And if *home* is that small snuggery
which limits the outer dark,
what bargains have we made here
in this forest of commodities, this
bright haven of inflexible sky,
where light fails, if at all,
late, and instantaneous, and always,
always on schedule?

Jazz

This is the night rain
brought down the ice dam
from my roof and the whole
damn gutter with it, Miles Davis
playing *kind of blue*
as the percussion
struck, a train derailing
against my house and I
went out to see
how water can twist
metal, a hollow serpent
with iceberg fins,
and I stood on the stoop,
rain in my hair, wind
up from the south,
and I remembered the notes
my father left, hand-inked
on a scratchy clef,
and how they played out his gift
for loneliness.

Fleurs d'Hiver

She photographs the tendrils, tails, the fans
night catches on her windowpane, the frost
of hexagons that bond and link till lost
in fields of ghostly wheat. Hydrogen
atoms join like this: quick when rough,
slow when polished facets slide away—
as light and lovers do—a winter's gray
malaise, composed of cold and breath.

And at that other window, pixels whir.
She transfers, crops, adjusts the brightness, hue,
finds forests, feathers, overblown mums,
landscapes she can save, or fix the blur
of petals that in time revert to dew
as hours sift to silence in her rooms.

Poem in Wartime

August 2003

Dark Sunday, and they are here again
on the chapel road: the triad of black
vultures, the tree's fractured trunk.

I park in the last open spot, summer
still simmering the air, vultures
between me and the drop-off

to the river, their heads gun-green
and stunted, their featherless wattles
shrugged against black bulk. I push

open the car door on a morning
I meant to pray, and some wire
vibrates from tree to nerve to hollow

at the back of my throat. Three times
they have been here, unholy tryst, and now
one spreads its sullen wings, one turns

its back; the third stares me down,
eyes indifferent as a munitions dealer,
a bag man when the payment's due. I tell

myself they are the clean-up crew,
undertakers of the wild, the ones
who drive the winged black hearse

across the sand, open for viewing
the flower of lung, the white satin skull.
But this is not the season

for pretty metaphors. This is a time
of mass graves undug in desert air,
bodies displayed for the booty they bring,

a time of war, hunched and waiting,
and a woman spooked on a Sunday morn
by creatures smaller, less potent than she

who will not budge as she steps from her car,
will not break their stare.

III. The X that Equals God

The First Year of Living Alone

Each day a cloister
in which the world slips away,
I keep this house
cusped on its hill
as I would keep an Alpine cell:
scissors, plate, a bowl of apricots
to catch the sun, a silence
in which I step through fear
into the room aloneness makes
and there lie down
unbridled, un-bride,
my body a narrow bed
as far from touch
as the moon from the branch of the pine.

How can I bear such solitude?
I will tell you:
in the first twilight
before the fireflies, children swing
in the park below. Girls
in sash-tied dresses
lean back, make streamers
of their hair, pump themselves
into a forgetfulness so pure
I rise in the air beside them,
become the voice
they streak through the dusk,
become the force that propels
even the lonely soul
to seek and gain the sky.

The Church Burning

for Fritz Pfotenhauer

Three a.m. and the gritty ring
of a telephone tells you: more than stars
ignite the sleep of late July. This is not the burning bush
you longed for. A frayed typewriter cord
brings you this message:
nothing is yours for very long.

The windows are giving witness when you get there:
Easter was light; Pentecost flame;
Elijah knew which chariots most like to mount the sky.

From the lawn you watch it all go upward:
twenty years of sermons, the recorded weight
of parish life, your grandfather's books
winging to ash, a wide-eyed Luther
with no thesis now except the one from physics:
heat rises, and loss is one way to ascend.

As morning comes, you stand more lightly
in the parking lot, vestments like smoky angels
strewn across the grass. You watch a bird,
its wings unblackened, climb a ladder of cloud,
a ladder of wind. You hold nothing in your hands,
nor would you. Above your head
clear air rises, turning and turning again.

Note

(to Carole Walton)

The wind-chime we bought
I have hung too high, too close
to the veranda wall,
its bright octave stilled
in all but craggy weather, its clean tones
coming as phantoms, memories,
countries long since gone: mere
birdsong in New Zealand's bush,
the call of a cloister bell, melodies
I have never heard, fingered
down a frequency lost to human ears.

Are there colors in a spectrum
we do not see? Small,
scrabbling dimensions
that elbow us into sudden pause,
a break in thought we can't explain,
a foot half-lifted as we wait
for something unsensed to fall?

And when we have purchased
out of the larger silence
a quiet concentrated
as stipples on the back of trout,
when sight fails, and hearing,
which is the last to go,
has eased us into the greater distance,
will light still reach us there?
Will the arc of the wind-chime's note
still go hurtling
through bright, now breathless, air?

Iris

in memory of Erskine Peters

Planning for springtime,
we traded roots, you with
a grocery bag of iris rhizomes,

I with small white stars
to twine the lattice of your fence.
Both of us were rife with digging,

unearthing tangled taproots
on other continents, framing
ancestors to line our walls.

But only you knew the songs
that sang those faces into history;
only you knew the weight

of every shade of leaf.
Now, in the drizzle of April,
I rake out my flower beds, feel

with numb fingers the aftermath
of winterkill, the consuming blizzard
that robbed you of your breath.

Summer will come this year
as usual, but what will bloom
is what you held up to the light:

iris is a trinity of fragile knowing;
iris is that which surrounds
the dark pupil of human sight.

The Glazier's Daughter

for Eva Mayer, 1823–1899

I am the product of sand,
a silica as silvery as the bits of air
the twilight stirs
into the cauldron of trees
on the far side of the river.

I am the red, molten glob,
the globe that breath expands,
the clear sheet that redefines
what is contained and what excluded.

They will tell you my eyes are crossed,
my vision not acute,
my soul a little peculiar.
But they do not know
that when I walk the fields
that rise beyond the vineyards—
potato, turnip, sugar beet—
I am my own secret:
that section of sky
the root-bound never see,
that solitude so pure
it melts into translucence;
silence as a crystal.

The Pyramid at Cholula

. . . why do you stand looking up to the sky?
—Acts 1:11

And when I walked there,
Toltec steps leading from a field
of marigolds (the hundred-petal flower),
and the church high above me—Señora
de los Remedios—I passed the peddlers
with their pottery, mud transformed,
earth itself a vessel, and I looked up
where unnamed peoples
built five pyramids, layered
like flinty overcoats, each over each,
skyward until the Spanish built
this bulbous dome
below the bulbous smoke
of the volcano Popocatepetl.

Four ages and four suns
already destroyed, the gods
gave a fifth world here,
here, where corn breaches the earth
with a reptile tongue,
where soft rain feathers down:
quetzal, bird of sky,
coatl, serpent of the ground,
Quetzalcoatl,
feathered serpent god.

And though for them salvation meant
the raising of a beating heart,
the puncture of a living tongue,
the double cowlick in a child's hair
marking his future sacrifice,
I circle with them
the double calendar
of desire and time, walk here
within the volcano's reach
as I have walked Iona, Assisi,
Yulara with its red, red rock,
walking out a hunger anywhere
stones are heaved upward,
the architecture tilted
toward the single prime,
toward the ultimate equation,
the voice beyond sound,
the *is* beyond our stories of it,
the X that equals God.

SELECTED POEMS

from *Brief Lives* (1981)

Elizabeth

(1868–1962)

I knew right then I was going to live—
grab life like a gunny sack
they said I was too small to hoist,
and not be picking it up in handfuls.
I told them that—that son and wife
who think because I'm ninety-four and fell
and something snapped besides the pickle jar,
who think I'll let go and die.
And I told that little one too,
winter nights when I had her to myself,
I told her I knew right then when the news came
and my sister only twelve,
stuck like a pig on that Wisconsin farm
of Uncle Jake's. That hired hand, come back
because he knew there'd be harvest cash,
and her home alone from church
with the baby sick. The baby watched
it all, they said, the cash box
and the ripping skirts, and the hog knife
when it struck, and he never touched
a hair on it. They say those young enough
shall live. And I was nine. And I took
my sister's years that never had time
to get the sweetness sucked out of them,
and I used them up and I used mine and
they think because I'm ninety-four
I'm done with it. And they don't know
no more than that slip of a girl
when I used to tell her how my sister died,
and how old lady Kressbach got it one night,
who used to run an inn by the Wilson store.
They say he done it with an axe

one night when the corn was all put up
and her notes past due, but they never
knew for sure about the axe
because he burned her to the ground,
and some damn fool—some deputy from town—
was trying to find blood stains when it
all cooled off, and everybody knew that
black skull was split in half in back.
I told her that—that little blonde one
whose cheeks were too pink for her not
to be messing in the rouge and her mother
said she never did, which nobody would believe.

And I told her, and those blue eyes
which she never got from her mother's side
would turn the color of her feedsack dress.
And I'd tell her about Heine Schmich
and how they put him in the State Pen
when he prowled once too often
around a barn with a gas can in his hand.
They figured it was him when the church went
on account of he worked for Uncle John
and that's who the gas can belonged to,
and everybody knew *he* never done it,
and knew Heine had it in for that young priest,
but not exactly why, because it happened
in the Penance box. And when John's barn
went, there wasn't much doubt no more.
And I told her that, before she run off
and joined the nuns for a spell,
which she hadn't ought to have done,
the last of my blood kin, putting her life
where I couldn't reach it, down some

dark hole likely full of bats and mice,
after she wouldn't even kill the gopher
that was getting my tomato patch,
and I told them that girl was too smart
for her own good, but no, they had to let her
take all the strawberry money out of
the savings account and buy one of them
typewriter things, and sit there
snapping letters on a page that sounded
like peas dropping into an empty pan
which she ought to have been shucking,
not old enough to button her own pants
and making up tales about girls murdered
in the hay, which nobody in their right mind
is going to believe, let alone sit down
and read it out of a book, and I told them
Lord knows where she gets that kind of nonsense
when she could have been helping me
with the raspberry canes and pulling out
the hairs around my mouth that never came
until the liver spots got bad,
like she did before she run off
and there's one life less around here,
which doesn't matter much because I got mine,
and they needn't think because I'm ninety-four
and something broke that I'm any worse
than my wedding clock, even if the face is stained,
when it still gets every minute down,
and I told them:

I know what's mine, by God,
and I'll take it while I live.

That Piece of Earth

i.

Old Mary Phillips had breakfast on the tombstones
when the living were not up; told passersby
it was all the same: she'd breakfast with the dead.
Sunny afternoons we watched her rise

from ditches, a sudden weed, viny baskets
trailing on her arm; found her camped
in our country church, snug as plaster saints,
her dresses hung in the vestry case, dishes

cropped like toadstools on the altar rail.
She denied burning candles, had no key.
Someone else had closeted those sooty stubs,
rearranged the flowers in the Ladies Aid bouquets.

A gaunt gray moth, she could slide through wood,
hover in flames no eye could see. No firebug,
she told them all—that time the sheriff came—
what burned on the altar was a sacred spark;

her body, a barricade, would swell into a stout
sod fence they'd have to cross. She knew
her ground, learned long ago:
through the earth is the way to the flame.

ii.

My friend says you are a messy potter, God.
In her hospital bed she knows
she's been kneaded wrong. Drugs
to slick down her mind glaze faces
that leer on the bathroom door. The nurse
sees nothing; her children bring posters,
cover the sneer, but she knows it's there.

                        I say
perhaps the fault's in the clay—or wood
that warped in growing long. Her kind lines
are hewn in a beauty she cannot see. Some things
are in the grain.

iii.

A scorpio, I learn from the charts
my region is water, but that's all wrong.
My father, who knows, would say it's earth.

He believes in the dust we'll return to;
taught us to plow around the slopes
rain strips of topsoil, to grow into the element
he'd conserve. He frowned on playing "ghost"

in the graveyard, petticoats like blight upon our heads.
White was better for daylight. Communion days
or Corpus Christi, farm mules, like heathen,
watched our processions from the fence. Two by two,

we were lilies behind a cross, our petals tossed,
our knees bent for the blessing of the Host.
I knelt one year on my grandfather's grave, my legs
shortened stems, white stockings staining in the sod.

I am the color of that clay turned windward,
those furrows where my father seeks the flame,
says we live by trust, take our seasons knowing
the part that's clay, the hand that goes back to the soil.

Rope Enough

the hay:

We were the penitentiary's best customer
that year my brothers made the rope machine,
buying bales of its hard-labor twine
to string the sweet loom of our alfalfa field.

A boy at each end, I was the bright bobbin
that coursed between the twisting strands,
blonde hair floating out and out with the running twine,

weaving rope strong enough to rip the flesh
from our father's hand that summer in the mow.
They grafted him in a body cast—a round white cup,
his elbow plastered for the handle's crook.

Looking back, I want to tip him,
pour out the pain that floated to his eyes,
let love be the pulley where he hitched that rope

to rafters in the shed, his own therapy,
pulled and pulled that handle of an arm
back to length and use. Three fates in that field,
we had measured out his pain, his health.

the belt:

This birthday,
I learn a sailor's art; tie down
one by one those strands that slip
and make my counting wrong.

I number back to strokes I've brushed
in my mother's hair—white threads
that multiply, snap like worms
as each part grows. She has seen hours
wriggle in the hand, dissolve into parts
before they die.

I pull this partial belt in line,
leave out the beads my friends advise
(I don't want what turns). Where string ripples
I pattern knot after knot, design
my defense. What I tie
stays.

the hanging:

Carol swallowed Mayo Clinic thread
the weeks her esophagus closed. Hand
over hand, like fishline, reeling in
and out again, it was all she had
against that sealing off.
Nights I wake to feel a closing,
a stricture in whatever goes within,
I hunt for pencils in the dark,
string out words across a page,
filament by filament, testing
until they're strong.
I know the old saying: *men given rope* . . .
I'm careful enough. I've seen friends
tangle in their words, dangle
where some capricious muse

hoists dreams on attic rafters, smashes
other loves, breathes the peace of oven doors
that open only once.

Wherever there's rope, there is danger;
I keep mine to the size of twine,
know that alone it won't hold me,
but it's there, tangled and dark by the bedside
nights I wake and swallow, swallow, hoping
it is enough.

Back Home in Indiana

for Ciaran O'Carroll

Were we to love in Indiana,
I would teach you
passions of the landlocked heart.
Groundswells would be swift
but languid. My body would part
from yours and level like a plain
where half-expected roadways curve.
Trucks would hurtle through the night.
The towns, when we came upon them,
would lie prone—sleepers unnerved
by a vast bed, unfiltered light.

                    Love,
far from glen and hawthorne tree,
you would shoulder the air
differently; would learn the trick
of the steady wheel; how to wear the heat
like a canvas glove, running miles
through your fingers like so much wheat.

You would go south
through an alphabet of towns
where children toss voices
from hedge to hedge at dusk;
westward, where Gary's great mouth
tears at the heartland's seams,
spits flame by night, steel by day.
You would learn that searing message well;

at every river's end, the sway
of corn leaves rasps out the dusty swell
of plump barns, well-fed sameness, the husk-
less truth of what we would be.

Were we to love here,
our coming would leave
no cleft in the day. Simple
as sheaves, our limbs would weld
nothing to this tempered land.
We would bed in the forge itself;
we would be the fired clay.

Plainsong for an Ordinary Night

The Amish sit down on nights of usual weather,
when nothing is wrong in northern Indiana
and nothing particularly right; when September
settles like a brooding hen, they sit and make
their plain and weekly letters for the *Budget* news:
In Salem, jars and cans are nearly filled with summer,

but the martins left, those busy days, before they knew.
Seed land has opened itself to winter wheat and weather,
and that stray rooster, pecking out the kernel of September
afternoons, will soon end up in the frying pan. Summer
was unkind to muskrats dead upon the road, and Indiana
wants slow-moving signs attached to every buggy made.

Nothing is particularly wrong in northern Indiana,
though Mary Luthy's finger sliced her summer
shorter, and Verna Kropf's grape jars exploded into news.
Mrs. Gabb's son went to drink and never got her coffin made . . .
but melons are rounding out the air of late September
the way marigolds flare up and fuel the dying weather's

fumes. Gardens are at the stalling point when summer
goes, but underneath the ground, parsnips swell and new
potatoes are fleshier than one expects in Indiana.
Lately, frosts have made a chaste, austere September,
but tonight, a bright moon shines. Youngfolks make
the most of days that linger. Courting buggies weather

ruts that drive older wheels to the shop. That new
horse of Fisher's spooked and skipped the bridge this summer;
the new wife had his ankle to soak and cows to milk whether
she liked it or not. The Alymer depot burned September
first; a load of hymnbooks and harness leather made
an unreined fire. And so things go in northern Indiana:

Mose F. Miller, 91, still steps off early September
walks as though morning itself might be something new.
Alma, who would have been 17, died this summer;
a load of bright, sliding hay blotted out the Indiana
sun too long, and her bees, without being told, made
honey dark, but sweet. Crows mourned the cooler weather.

Toward morning, a steady September rain will weather
out the end of summer. Libations of cider will be made.
And the Millers of Goshen, Indiana, will pluck the late beans like
    news!

Auction

They are selling my afternoons
stacked up like saucers on the lawn,
my doilies, sewing chest, my coffee pot.

"A fine antique," proclaims the man
with the megaphone face, and the bed
my babes were born in—is gone—

is gone. The heat seams me indoors.
They sell my quilts, what pieces
of flesh and dark I can still recall.

They sell the walnut chest of drawers.
I did not tell them: the mottled mirror
is where the woman lives. I saw her

one twilight, dressed in my wedding face,
with a single jewel I never owned.
Certain nights I rose and could not sleep:

she was Spanish, a duchess, a mermaid,
eyes stippled like a trout stream,
pupils chipped from water and time.

I dared not tell how I floated to join her,
my joints liquid as lamp oil, in a country
far as childhood, a fragrance light as tulle.

Now they check for dovetailed corners,
pry at my life for loose veneer.
When the money is counted, they will

load the old lumber of my bones
in a wheelchair, store me in a sterile
lumber room. She will not store so easily.

Once only she spoke, like water
sucking down a stone. "Hush," she said.
"It has been decided. I will not go

when they take you. They will sell
what is solid. I am breath, darkness,
the essence of rain. I am what stays,

do you hear me? I am what remains."

Two Letters

(from letters of Georg Hornung)

i.

Winona, Minnesota
January 1, 1868

Much beloved children:

Yes, time goes—I have to write
the days, the months, the years.
The 63rd year of my age is close
and mother's 62nd.
Leisebeth has, since the end of October,
a little daughter; Christina's family too
is well and cheerful. Their harvest is good:
600 bushels of wheat, and food enough
for people and cattle. Peter builds
a new house; by spring the lumberwork
will soon be ready.

We have a covered farm, no lack
of wood, a house halfway to the water.
Our kitchen and cellar is full, much
cabbage and turnips. We have raised
and killed a good pig of 250 lbs. I make
a good wooden fence; a field of winter
wheat stands wonderful within it.

Only one mishap done last fall:
a prairie fire came and burned a haystack.
Our new neighbor did it—a brother-in-law
to Eva Knapp. He made a fire in his clearing.

Today it starts to snow again a little,
but not cold; we have a sleighing way.
Please let me hear from you.

your very loving father

ii.

Rochester, Minnesota
September 2, 1869

Much beloved children:

I am much pleased to hear from you,
especially that the grandchildren write
so beautifully. O my dear ones, you
are inviting me to visit in Ohio. It
would pleasure me much, but the railroad
took so much from me for fifty miles,
how would I stand it for days? And this:
I do not like to leave mother's grave.

I have sold my land: 28 hundred dollars.
The buyer will pay 20 hundred if they build,
next to the cemetery by Philips', a new church.
I do not like to be hard in this matter;
mother and Christina are there.

After I collect in October the remainder
of my money, I consider Ohio. The interest
I give to Joest for the trouble I caused;
I have only to pay the doctor
a hundred more.

News here is not so pleasant:
a man three weeks married, killed by a
Sioux, a board thrown at his chest. 18 miles
from Winona, a baby is missing. Indians
are suspected. The child was alone—the parents
in the field. Weather is hot. Thunderstorms
cause damage on the railroad and crops.

I close now.
This from your loving father, written
with trembling hand. I will not
be able to do much longer.

Margins of the Map

*The writers crowd the countries of which they know nothing into
the farthest margin of their maps. . . . All beyond this is portentous
and fabulous, inhabited by poets and mythologers, and there is
nothing true or certain.*

—Plutarch, "Life of Theseus"

I was seven
when they made me learn the names
of oceans, continents, colored shapes
like boots and fists, and fat split plums
tossed into the sea. I traced inlets green
as a lost mother's eyes.

   "Here," they said,
"you shall live. Here is your bed—
(this white tablet standing gravely in a row).
Here is your desk, your bowl, the orphan's prayer
to be said in unison. All days are charted.
Here you will save your soul."

At seventeen, they showed me
to the parlor where he sat. "We will take
one horse," he said. "Salt for preserving
and an iron pot. There may be wolves. And cold.
It is known there are rivers there.
All else is beyond the markings of the map."

"I have no dowry," I said, "not a dish
I can call my own." "The sky
will be a deep new bowl," he said,
"your mouth a cup."
I said: "I will go."

High in mountains, he pulled the cloth
from my own small peaks, taught me crevasse
and hidden canyon—a joyous plunge to silky lakes
my body did not know. On awesome plains,
he rose, and blood swept through me
like the wind through rising grain. I vowed
the land was ours; began to swell with seed.
I said, "We will mark this place,"
but his eyes looked past me through the fire, marked
small eyes that began to circle and shine.

I remember nothing
of when it started. Both of us ate the meat,
drank deeply from streams. His breath grew hotter
in the night; he threw off clothes, returned
too late from hunts; I would awake
to fire in the night. I would call
but his fired eyes would not be seeking mine.

We moved always to newer lands,
shaggy as his face. Soon he would not drink;
words came out in foam. The last night,
wolves gathered, circled thrice. He rose,
pierced their circle with a single thrust,
and raised his snout like a border line.

Now the howling is done. I have burned
the old map. I make new lines while a round moon
traces how my belly swells, new promontory
on the body's well-tracted land. If I live
and this child lives, we shall leave records
before going on.

You who read this,
will have come as far as we have gone.
You will have crossed the boundary of certainty.
You will be walking the plane
that we have walked. Here,
all that is
is true.

Moon for My Grandmother's *Grand'mère*

They did not
even list your name—those fathers
of my father who inked out my heritage,
naming sons and husbands, an issue
of farmers, not poets, on those blank Bible leaves.

But I have pieced you out; have made
you a name from the stirring in my blood,
a face from words that roam like cattle
through my sleep. When the moon has pulled
at my body, I have known you well.

Bred to breed sons for the plow,
you slipped that harness one winter night
halfway from barn to milkhouse; flung out
your pails where the moon touched the snow;

oblivious of night, his arms, of the babes
who sucked you dry, you whirled in that foam,
caught the white spray full on your full-mouthed face,
murmured, "Soul, O my soul!" to the moon.

Entrance Day

i.

Ten years ago
I rode these river hills too fast
in rain my mother
thought would cause an accident,
driving to demand whatever lay
behind the high and cloistered walls.

All of us were calm; my father
just forgot his wallet, brother retold jokes.
My mind numbed itself
on items from the clothing list:

> a metal trunk from Sears
> a laundry bag
> seven bars of soap
> nylons (black) in boxes
> plain stationery, pins . . .

ii.

Sister Mira let us in;
stone like great veined mirrors
watched our steps. A nameless nun
fluttered with the bags, our wraps, her scapular
(My brother said, "How *do* they get those things
around their heads?"), ushered us
through parlors other families occupied
like frightened troops. A Nebraska girl,
sheep-eyed and grinning out her fear,
picked handles on her purse to shreds.

The rest was quick:
they fed the families pie, packed
us off to fitting rooms ("Postulants
wear garb modest, ample, plain . . .")
collected money, makeup, cigarettes,
sent us out to say goodbye.

The family left; I did not cry.
I read *Pax et Bonum* high in stone.
A novice said, "That's peace and good."

iii.

At evening prayer
behind the novice rows, white-veiled
and straight as laundry pins,
silence was the final cloister door. I felt it
as I feel autumn, tangy and breathing smoke,
pull me out of summer,

                     and I feel it now—
a counterpull to flesh. I ride in rain
the glazed green summer of these river hills
and I do not touch. It is as though

anchorites bend to touch the sand
in the scorched, restless autumn of my bones.

The Bats

That houseful of nuns had no belfries
but fourth-floor attic eaves were close enough
to deliver baby squirrels in spring and bats
in any weather. Summer nights

we stoked our silence with the humid air,
waited for the first barrage of slamming doors
to see night gowned nuns arise with brooms—
ghosts of crusades past—brandish dust mops,

night-veils, books, exorcise with backhand strokes
the winging dark. A fat nun says
tennis rackets make the surest hit
(Superior says a frying pan); I know

my mettle—I hide; conjure thoughts
of the nun who woke, black wings
inching up her chest. (One gray and furry dawn
two were in the pocket of her robe.)

I don't buy that business of "harmless
mice with wings." I've had gargoyle faces
swoop through my transom as I'm stuffing
rugs in the door. I don't like darkness
zeroing in.

I fear some night in dreams
I'll take to the streets, wing out my mantle
and fly. One never knows what caves
lurk high in bat-lined dark. Those quivering walls
are close. I feel a draft within.

For the P.O.W. in My English Class

The images ricochet.
In the third row, you are not safe
from Sartre's firing squad. The trial held
has said we all must die. I offer flowers
from the Judas tree. The flowers turn to poppies,
their slashes into blood. I am the first
to confess my crime: I didn't know that you would come:
I have mined the room with my reading list.

You come with the others across that field,
make it look easy when nothing explodes—
(You've dodged things before; your timing is good.)
Like Hemingway trout, you steady yourself
in this flow of words, take with the current
those burnt-out years, the trees, the blossoms,
the swamp you know too well to fear.

Lieutenant, your journal opens
like a flower torn in half. Words drop;
the stamen, petals split. In this zone,
it doesn't matter if the pollen burns my skin.
I am looking for what holds us both to earth;
I am looking for a root, a stem.

Practicing

To sign for a single passport
is one way to begin. To take
any journey alone. To be the one
who finds the body on the beach,
eyes splintered like the agate chips
that will wrap around the neck
of every dream. These are ways of practicing.

To walk through autumn without love,
to count in spring what has winter-killed,
to rejoice in late flowers,
dried fruit. In strange countries,
to peer into the boiling pot and watch
dark hands take the turtle from the shell;
to choose the suit for the burial.

The rest are simpler ways:
to lie back as a woman lies
awash in the bedclothes with love—
to feel the bouy of self
slip far from the hand; to trust
the blackness before the surgeon's knife,
colors fleeing like birds
in summer's wake. To step into a storm
and give freely of your breath
for every breath the wind will take.

These are the trial runs.
When the great lightness comes
like a door opening out of the body
or a core falling, swift and aglow,
you will be ready to bite down hard.
You will remember all that has left you.
And then you will go.

Four Novembers: An Aviary

i.

Each birthday
something of you flies in.
First, it is a lakeside song,
your fingers waking like wings
against my face;
then, at dusk,
a piece of wood
I stoop to toss
from the parking lot:
it is a carrier pigeon
grave and dying.

Next morning,
fog.

ii.

I return from the airport
to a starling down the chimney,
roosting on the drapery rod,
rapping, tapping at my chamber door.
His eye alone will stir the dust,
tangle the wisps of my hair.

He has one song:
       a winged thing
       breaks whatever holds it
       evermore.

iii.

The snowy owl
can see all of Chicago
without changing perch.
The head pivots
on the bearings of his eyes.
He knows there is no one beside me.
I believe he has no past,
no neck,
no bone.

iv.

The end when it comes
is often in a letter.
I visit the friend
whose brain nestles tumors,
read the numbers
on the bandage round her head.
She is dated like a package,
a postmark that says
she can never return.

Home through the park,
I give your letter
to whatever wind will take it.
November has no birds.
I watch the pieces sail.

To Speak a Word of Grief

for A. K. O.

I said nothing when your death
came in the mail. Waves
that would not hold you
floated through telephone cords
and washed my rooms with a quiet
so stiff it might have been
your hand. Seven months are gone.

Now I push north through Michigan
knowing that you chose to die. Leaves
raise their veins to a splendid knife;
tendrils stiffen; rain waits in the west.
A friend has written you a letter;
it returns postmarked: low tide.

"I have written to a dead man," he says,
like the chorus to a song. "I have
written to a dead man," plays louder
than the radio, plasters the billboards
of these small towns, shines from the stands
of roadside fruit.

I am writing to a dead man, I say
as Michigan vineyards die leaf by leaf.
I have not forgiven the words
you did not harvest, the small, hard
grapes you pitched into the sea.
To speak of love would be to swallow
all that silence—that gathering
of water, pain and fruit.

I bless/curse these syllables
you left me. My mouth bells
like a hollyhock. These words
will no longer wait.

What I Did This Summer

(an essay in two parts)

i.

I foreswore love for the season;
there is less to regret in domesticity.
Lone and lazy, I kept a reasonable

house, stripped old paint from various
limbs (a sluggish brew), made designs
on the future of my cane-bottom chairs.

I hauled down the trunk my past was shipped
in, tried to remember my former names.
To reduce clutter, I ground up the news, chipped

daily deaths and marriages, old dog-eared
wars, into a pure gray pulp, a bone-
clean sheet on which to bed my rumpled fears.

In short, I slept alone.

ii.

I relaxed. All that remained was to nail
down this peace. But plants I put out
to summer came back matted, full of snails.

My prize butterfly was attacked by moths;
a soft, slow worm bred in the windows
of its wings, a destruction tender as cloth.

Now the twilights all come earlier. They make
sequins of paint peeling from the porch.
Like the way you kissed my thumbnail, I thought.

That was my first mistake.

To Close a House

for C. H.

To close a house
is to be more sure of distance;
to measure off the days we did not count,
the length of rugs, of ivy vines, the tensile strength
of words that form the linkage we have left.

We have packed and shipped what's over.
Your goldfish swim in their traveling pail,
the phone in a disordered sleep. Disconnected thoughts
pull in and out; I have turned off the gas;
the bills are paid; the clock

ticks off the space I've yet to move in.
Like a child, I try to adjust my pulse,
my breathing. I say your name
in the rhythm of its beat. A last time
I turn the kitchen faucet. The old leak
still gathers—a globe that forms and falls.
I wait to see it shatter, but the water holds,
the ticking holds; I cannot hear my heart.

The house is closed and I must be the mover,
the pendulum that changes space to time.
I breathe and hunt a span to hold me.
I move my hands;
I start the clock.

from *Women at Forty* (1988)

Women at Forty

Women at forty wear their skin
like phases of the moon, like
crescents of pleasure bent to catch
all angles of light: the slippery
solstice, the fragile truce of noon.

Fresh from sleep, they are assured
that yesterday's paleness was but a sag
of light, an inconsequent fading.
Yet they wear their fullness conscious
of its snagged regrets, the lines
that web against the blooming.

Women at forty afford the dark side.
As the womb grows tighter,
they learn the shift in the lover's eye,
his taste for firmer flesh,
the secrets he is still avoiding:
again and again, they've kissed the skull
beneath the lover's grin, know
as surely as they know his thrust,
that what is full will soon be waning.

When sadness comes, women at forty
go without fear to a shuttered room,
bless themselves, bed down believing
that each effacement is but a rest,
a teasing dark before they ride again,
pushing the clouds from their right-of-way,
pulling the sea behind them.

The Picture Bride

(Because the first wave of Japanese immigration, 1880–1900,
was almost entirely male, numerous marriages were arranged through
photographs prior to the woman's immigration.)

In the beginning, I said "Seattle"
like a sound that could ferry me
inside its womb from Kobe to Yokohama
where Fuji floated like the hope
that had led me to the sea.

I sailed on the *Minnesota,* a stranger
name, and I sail it still when
infant voices divide my sleep as dawn
divides the curtains of this one-room
house. The photograph sleeps
in a peach crate, the husband in bed
where I bring him the tea, the choicest
scallions, the garments he once wore
to smile at a lens.

He clothed me in ambition
the day the ship touched land:
a high-necked blouse, button shoes,
a corset to lace out the air
of Yokohama. I could not bend;
the department-store lady
slipped bloomers on my nakedness:
a western bride.

Then I bent above the cabbages,
the berries, acres of squash,
the pain of drawing water
three days past the birth. Sometimes

when I rise to light the fire,
I watch my husband sleep, a silt
of satisfaction covering his face.
I could never tell him

I am back at the rail, the ship
nudging a shaggy shore, my heart
a morsel I keep from gulls
who wheel and cry: *return, return* . . .

The darkness of my body is mine again,
and I close my eyes, sink
from the surface of the photograph,
from the moment I must open on the dock,
the fir trees, the lapping Sound,
the smiling men with photographs

—on that one still face
that will fix at the back of my eyes,
the image I must hold forever.

First Notice

The words are gone. It is that,
more than the other slippage—
the missing glasscase,
the iron left on—that troubles her.

Once, words were like a train,
an express that rumbled through her sleep,
a passenger line that was never late,
hurling across the borders
she needed to cross, bearing
her hopes, her quantity of luggage.

She is not really old; her brain
is too stable for that disease
which takes all names away,
but last night she could not think
what it was that held her eggs.
Kettle? Spider? Cast-iron box?
—a word as transient as the Zephyr
rolling out to Watertown, as the man
who left his brakeman's hat . . .

Sometimes she sees faces
blur like a window gathering speed,
finds photos of those vanished
from her Christmas card list.

Sometimes she dreams
she stands in a station
ready to board. The conductor
swings down the little stool-steps,
reaches to take the bag from her hand,
becomes—in a puff of steam—
something for which there is no name,
something that eyes her coldly, says:
Your ticket is expired, Ma'am;
this is not your destination.

Artifacts

One lover left her a thimble,
another a stone. This one brings
a cut-glass plate, flowers so transparent
they might be mixed with rain.

She keeps such things in a cedar box:
old buttons, charms, notes that wash up
at the edges of life, a lockless key,
a leaf she found in a geography book.

She keeps them as solids, as ballast,
mornings when time floats away
—as thirty years before her father kept
rusty horseshoes, sleigh bells in decay.

His sister left a single bed,
a hoard of stamps, a tiny sewing kit.
Stirring hankies in their lilac dust,
she wondered: can you make a life of this?

Now, when love is shaky, when the telephone
brings news of death from a fading house,
she hunts poems, pearls, the cut-
glass plate, the work she would want

remembered. Before the window
she fingers them: feather, shell,
a stalk of bittersweet—consoled by weight,
by stasis. When she is calm enough
she will think of things she did not save:

an afternoon cottage by water
a lift of curtains in the wind
words that hover like a dragonfly
in blue fluorescence
his lips grown silent—
transparent, blue-etched wings.

Beneath Annie's Gown

Anna Storcy
Hartford, Michigan
1823–1904

At first, it mattered little that she had no past.
Things washed up from the Civil War,
even in the North: a rifle butt,
a piece of uniform, a peg-legged
woman who could hold her own
at the cider mill, the blacksmith shop,
trading jokes in the gristmill crowd
until some clumsy neighbor brushed her skirts
and the sudden stillness round her mouth
became as dense as the grinding stone.

We were used to minor oddities.
We bought her flour, drank
cider from her press, ate the tartness
of her apple cakes at the Catholic Aid bazaar.
We made light of those who said
she was a fugitive, a pirate's moll, a murderess
with one leg tied up, skirts a clandestine cave
to which someone knew the route.
All of them were wrong.

The day she died, she sucked down silence
like water from a gourd,
the stone of her breath
harder than that other stone,
Francis Keasey's mortuary slab,
where eighty years of secrets all came clear:
the penis, the withered testicles,
the pale and flagging pendants of what she had denied.

Then we remembered everything:
the too-large hands, the furtive smile,
50-pound kegs tossed easily as onion sacks . . .
It might have been a gold-rush scheme, we said,
the plot to kill Lincoln, the psychopath
who chunked pieces of his wife into the Finger Lakes,
babies in the well . . .

But some of us were never sure.
We woke beside dreamers
whose distance was farther
than any night could go,
stood alone at a window of empty stars
and knew what we had always known:

beneath Annie's gown
was what we all possessed:
a spare and shrouded, unrepleted, still unfathomed
heart.

This Lesson

*Each piece of writing has taught me how to write it but was
of no use for the rest.*

—Eudora Welty

I am back again in that forbidden house,
the stairway a backbone of oak, the rooms
awash with ancient light. "Look around,"
they say, and I peer into closets,
pull hats from shelves, lift out
corsets, cloaks—a freedom
they may not have intended.

The drawers are full of someone's past,
a sentence that begs to be finished.
I thrust both hands into drowsing silk;
a cocker spaniel barks;
in another room, a bowl
is broken . . .

I search for parchment
(the oldest skin) in the rolltop desk,
find pencils instead, but something's wrong:
they are sealed, unsharpened, blunt
as a skull, a palisade of yellow staves
to warn me. Footsteps knock

against the staircase. I cannot move.
Voices come from nowhere, an argument
of sense with light. They call
another's name. "Go up," they say,
"to the attic . . ."

Possum

With blood down one side
and a tail thick enough
to whip the sap from trees,
he blots the morning sun
from my front walk,
turns a woeful snout
to look at me
then ambles like a drunk
across a dozen feet of lawn,
eyes focused on a country
that is either far or deep.

"Under the neighbor's porch,"
I say over the phone,
"hurt—or rabid—
looking for a place to hide, I think,"
but when the rescue van comes,
flashlights and poles assembled,
nothing stares back
from that shuttered womb;
nothing plays dead
in the earth-scented privacy,
the easeful dust
I thought that he was aimed for.

"I was sure he'd seek darkness,"
I say in defense,
but the woman points,
and there he is again,
claiming the lawn
in sunshine public as a courthouse square,
waiting while we move the cage,
then stepping up to the rubber noose,
offering his head . . .

Some wounds are like that.
They hound us out of the hiding place,
eat away the normal cloak
of decency,
leave us standing in sunlight,
with traffic going by,
leave us saying: Look, look!
Stop your cars!
This is real.
This is what happened.
I want you to believe this.
And I do not want to die.

Taps

The man against the fence is waiting for the gun.
He has been here since morning, a pale stump
in a line of old oak posts. It may go cheap,
he thinks—the bidding's slow, the field's
not shaded, the auctioneer's too old.

He gestures toward the graveyard down the road:
we'd all be there if the Krauts kept coming—
that's why he wants it—maximum deterrents
and safety in a shoulder load. He'd vote
to build more missiles any day. I tell him

I am waiting for a chest that locks, a safe,
a place to hold things—for birds whose song
will never fail the air. The auctioneer
keeps chanting; a small vase blooms, blue-veined
against the sky. Around us, shadows slip.

The bugled chant is waning: the day is going,
going . . . The notes are gone. We are standing
in a field that still exists. We are waiting
for the final bid, the last salute. We are waiting
for the guns.

Getting through Sundays

for Arthur Oberg

The ghosts of Sunday are small.
Even as a child you felt the gap
in the afternoon, the restlessness
you could not exorcise, tipping dominos
in your grandmother's house, the men
snoring in their chairs, the women smiling
like sisters-in-law. It was a space
too pale to be labeled grief, a concave fret
of something missed, as though
you knew in advance the lovers
you'd lose, the clocks that would tick
long past their last winding. Once

in a high coastal town, the future
beckoning across the bright water,
you waited through Sunday anesthetized,
while up in the turret, a window dropped,
trapped a hundred butterflies
who died there in the sun.
The next day was dark.
You swept frail and folded corpses in a dustpan,
threw splinters of flight to the wind.

Now you listen to the radio,
to rain that falls on all of Indiana.
You pick dead leaves from your plants,
think of all the letters you owe,
and how strange you feel—as though
some hollow behind your eyes
were suddenly enclosed—as though
under your skin, vaporous wings
stirred, stuttered awake, and rose.

Letter to an Insomniac

Suppose you took a different street
the day of the accident. Suppose
you fell through water
instead of glass, your ribs
folding like petals, the air
unruptured, the day intact.

Suppose you let the phone ring
one rainy night, the door wide open.
The man you jilted last year returns.
Suppose his fingers have sharpened;
suppose a knife in his voice.

Suppose you took that plane
from Chicago—the DC-10
that flew straight into news.
Or suppose, in the airport,
you sit next to a stranger
with frost-bitten eyes. Suppose
he kisses you, offers you marriage
or money, a job on the pipeline.
Suppose you packed nothing
you'd care to bring back.

Suppose you do not read this.
Suppose you never admit
what your waking denies:
all choices are final
but only one is your last.
Think of yourself on a train
going westward, the tracks
suturing up your past. Night
flows over like water; the window
gives you nothing back; the berth
is coffin-sized . . .

It is not what you think.
It is Nebraska or North Dakota,
nothing darker. Suppose
you believe me. Morning
will come, stations spring up
in the thistles. Suppose you sleep.
The line will continue.
The conductor will wake you
before the last stop.

Family History

My mother will not say "the pigs
ate out the bricks" in those years
so lean there was no turnip blood
and cold snouts sucked a clay foundation.

Old aunts scowl through her prose,
and she writes: "The house
had to be abandoned; bricks crumbled . . ."

She lists dates, years, siblings
tumbled like a wagonload of beets
(though she does not say it)
out of muffled darkness, small
disturbances in sleep. She writes
a clean and tidy record.

My mother does not say she stood
as I see her, slim girl on the plains
of too much sorrow—the crumbled house,
the hatchery gone, the father's death
rounding her mouth like a stone

—does not say she left that graying house
while a spotted sow, her teats gone slack,
her nostrils dusty, moved toward a foundation
I see clearly now, sniffing out
the blood of a house, rooting, rooting . . .

Little Sisters

This birthday I have reached the age
where my mother bore
the last of her dead daughters—
one that was whisked away
before its first clean cry
could scour the naked room, the later two
a blue that refused to brighten.

"Baby Girl, Infant Daughter of . . ."
the little markers said,
and I listened from behind the stove
in her last pregnancy,
watched her body swell and sag,
knew from the shape
of those whispered words
that something was amiss—
she was weighted already
with two small stones.

Summer mornings I called them forth—
the little sisters I had never seen—
made them faces
from the old ache
in the air above the garden,
hair like mine
from the grassy space
where root crops should have been.

I learned of blood tests, transfusions,
a factor called Rh,
my little sisters
dreaming their aquatic days
on lethal ropes, my mother
almost dead.

Now at the kitchen table
lighting candles on a cake,
I am empty-handed,
empty-wombed,
no daughters to give her
as she counts again
my miraculous birth,
fourth and forceps-born,
her last survivor in that war
of blood with family blood.

I reach for her hand and hold it,
but there are spaces here,
tender lacunae we cannot fold away.
Still somewhere the hand-stitched garments,
the gingham quilts, the counting game.
Still the soot-smudged corner
where I crouched beneath the stovepipe
and fingered like a rosary
the small pebbles of their names.

Dust

The sky was a plate of curds
the autumn Uncle Reuben came, three days late
in the afternoon mail. His mortal whey
gone to thin smoke above a southern town,
he came north stamped, insured,
delivered RFD to the roadside box
where my mother waited. Nothing
inside but a plastic bag, she said,
and closed it. Kept him
in the cool front room
till prairie skies glazed blue,
a plate washed clean and empty,
and the priest could come.

My parents refused
to distribute the ash—
they will nothing to scatter—
the posthole digger drew a tidy plug,
a sweet core of grassland,
and they dropped him in.

Augering into another autumn,
I remember his smile, his scars from the fire
at the dry cleaning plant. I put down
tulips between the hard frosts,
crocus bulbs with absurd little navels . . .

And so the story ends: no flesh to decay,
no bones to toss up centuries later—
only a woman with a trowel in hand,
only this wind
across the edge of Indiana, this swift
and gritty eddy of leaves,
a scent, perhaps, of something relinquished,
sand in the mouth,
a speck in the eye.

The New Appliances

First there was the stove
the year his heart went bad,
a new Maytag after the Monarch range
simmered thirty years off their electric bill.
Then the Christmas we all could sense
something was amiss: a gassy smell,
a scent like danger, perhaps like death,
worn-out valves no longer pumping warmth
through rooms where she stokes him daily
with low-salt food like the doctor said.

After the new furnace, the microwave:
meals in a flash, she says,
plenty of time to count the pills
in the minutes that his oatmeal cooks.
Then, last month, the stroke.

It was hardly anything, she says:
a brief ungluing of eyes,
words that stuck, food that tumbled
from the left side of his mouth.
He is well enough to go to town
when they choose the new wash machine,
automatic, a real time-saver,
no more rinse tubs, no cellar steps to climb,
no more wringers for his old gray socks,
fibers thinning beneath her very hand.

It's the new pipes from the wellhouse
make all the difference, she says,
—as though years were a cistern
she could bypass when dry—
And you should get yourself a freezer, she says,
and try those herbed salt-substitutes.
Such good flavor, she says,
like spring coming right out of the garden again,
like water when we could drink it
straight from the well.

The Many Kinds of Doubt

i.

First, there was the river.
Dark July, and you led me down.

Fish-flies littered the streets about us,
dove at our feet in their eagerness to die.
In my childhood town, they bulldozed
them from the bridges, slippery death
drifting like the empty hulls of snow.

Here you took my hand,
moved from the shadow of the bridge
to the shadow of the pilings.

It's safe, you said. Come down.

ii.

We waited out Christmas
the year we couldn't leave; windchill
a minus 87, and every pipe
its own icy wreath. At dinner
in the only restaurant open, we burned
the brief fuel of what there was to say. Did you
have turkey as a child? Did your children
like their gifts? Does adultery
give the injured one an unquestioned right to leave?

No one was going anywhere. We split
the bill and left. How often
do vagaries of weather
immobilize the heart?

iii.

I would be a better Christian
(you say) if I'd leave the saving
to someone else. Like these nights
we hear traffic behind the plaster,
the spill of something crumbling overhead.
Squirrels in the attic, you say,
and go off to sleep, but it's more than that:
something scrapes and gnaws
the wires that used to connect.

This is the difference between us:
when trouble comes,
one of us sleeps and one of us wakes,
one of us rests and one of us rises,
tapping the walls in a white flannel gown,
listening at corners, testing the sockets
that have started to spark.

One of us dreams and one of us watches,
knowing what the dreamer fears:
that some night the other will descend the stair,
begin to strip paper from the living room,
dismantle the lights, pull out
the bricks one by one
with her own hands, until she finds
the beast in the wall, until she has torn
the whole house down.

Things Come in from the Cold

These shortened days
I wake to cold, to wasps like snow
against the window where they whine
a frantic nest into the eaves.

Things come in from the cold
in autumn. Crickets comment on my sleep.
They have claimed the cellar,
the coal-bin; the field mice

have claimed last season's shoe.
One clear morning, wings break
inside the chimney—something falls.
You tell your son:

in autumn things fulfill themselves.
"You mean they die," he says,
and there it is again: that field
of goldenrod bending, the lines

you trace on my palm, that spider
dropping from a single thread. You take my hand
although we have no hope
the seasons will stop spinning—

that leaves will cling, green and wet,
or the old worm turn more slowly.
"—But come in," you say,
and for a time, however brief,
winter is only a softer light,
and across the ice, we see distance glowing.

Playing the Bells

Five stories up, we climb the steeple to play
this carillon against the dusk, against the rain
that returns us to darkness as surely as to day.

In a tar-papered room, you sit and sway
above levers like spools, like a loom ordained
to music. Five stories up, where we climbed to play

these spindles of sound, I poke through the splay
of dust: droppings, bottles, dead pigeon remains—
a presage of darkness as surely as of day.

Then "Alouette" rings above the hymnal's gray
tones, your sudden whimsy, and I strain—
five stories up, in the steeple where you play—

to hold it longer, to keep this bright foray
against October's dying, against the twilight pain
that turns us toward darkness more surely than toward day.

Notes ending, I will the resonance to stay—
to be stronger than twilight, stronger than rain,
five stories up in the steeple where we play
against the turn of darkness, believing surely in the day.

Geese Crossing the Road

Winter again,
and the heart chokes down a little,
driving mid-country, the windshield
an esplanade of rain.

Past prairie towns
scattered on the soil like ancient vertebrae,
I slow the car for a farmer's geese,
a haughty promenade, not to be hurried
as they step out their scorn
of rain, each feather in place,
feet glowing like a beacon.

In another town, you are less secure
than they, wearing my troubled love
like an ill-stitched coat
against such rudiments of weather.

Dear heart,
whatever grief I've caused you,
the truth is this: love at midlife
is not flight, not
buoyant migration to another plane,
but small journeys, sudden
new species of touch, a proud arc
in the lifting neck, a stay
against depletion. It is these geese
crossing the road, calling us back
to some primordial attention
we had wandered from, some forgotten state
where we too touched the earth
and stepped out the essence
of whiteness, of sureness, of morning.

Ice Climber

Lake Michigan, March

I have followed you into a land
not land but frozen as a dream
might freeze the last wakes of longing
or a photograph might still the cliffs
of storm from breaking on the beach.

You point to fault lines, cleavage,
the face of an ice-cliff about to break,
but I follow in your steps
climbing the pock-marked waves,
slipping down an icy swell
thirty feet above a concave sea.

Below us, waves create new caverns,
ice floes bounce like flagstones afloat.
"We are walking on the moon," I say.
"No," you say. "We walk a tideless sea."

You tell me again of danger:
what is shining will not stay.
But we are standing in sunlight,
the ice floes rustle like leaves.
A breeze touches my hair as you
might touch, as though time too
could solidify, and seasons from now
we could still be here,
riding this crest to the sea.

The Moment of Loss Is Always Familiar

The moment of loss is always familiar:
it is the first breath drawn
outside the hospital room, the dull
menstrual ache of expulsion, the step
you miss down a stairway of rain,
the letter you find months later.

It's the moment you wake
and know something's wrong: the crib
is empty, the windshield's cracked,
the lining ripped out of everything.
It's the miscarried winter when ice
breaks the eaves, when you dream

you are back in that field,
the cattle astray, the farm lights receding.
Owls are swifter than soft, pulsing fur,
and you run, run through the heart of the corn,
each tassel exploding, each leaf
a sharp-tongued sneer: Who? How long?

Loss is the moment you stand still
in that field, the wind dropped,
the cattle gone. Sound, like a heartbeat,
has ceased, and you are the space
the wind has removed, you are
the loss, the one no one is seeking.

What If a Woman

forty-three years old and
driving her car down the street
just after the lover
who accused her of terrible things
had found another girl
and sunlight was scaling
the tavern roofs
and spring stood in the trees
a silk-winged Icarus
ready to leap
and she whispered to herself
"I am alone
alone
and I will not tell
how lovely it is
I will not tell
anyone at all"
and she floated right up
through the roof of the car
right into the folds
of the silk-winged sky
above a dozen maple trees
unleafed as yet
who leaned back to watch
and applauded?

Different Stars

I am learning the meaning of *antipodes,*
the opposite, the polar star,
a day gone from life
as the plane skims the date line
then all direction gone.

It's not the left-hand driving,
not the telephone dial I turn from below.
Cold blows up from the south here;
water goes down the drain hole
the other way round.
In May's quickening dusks,
time is the truest vertigo,
June a bright winter
where yellow leaves fall past camellia buds
and cabbage trees
fake their way into being palms.

I can fake nothing,
not a knowledge of streets,
not a knowledge of stars
these cold June nights
I stand beneath a sky turned round,
the hunter askew,
the bear herself
all out of joint . . .

Across the Tasman Sea,
the Northern Crown
becomes a boomerang—
a lofty throw
from the Dreaming Time.
Here the Milky Way,
that basket of stars,
that long white shark,
is Tane's net staked out
on Rangi's cloak—
old Father-Sky
whose dark embrace
once covered Mother-Earth
with night.

We become what we believe,
the stories we tell
to make the random right.
It is the reason for war,
for failures at love,
for all that occurs
under different stars,
each of us
our own coordinates,
sure of our latitudes,
sure that this time
the ball's in the net,
the arrow's slung,
the one right tale
that will speak our lives
is here and has begun.

A Legend

In the Dreaming Time,
kangaroo men and wallaby men
had faces that carved themselves
on the face of the Rock:
skull, brain, the spilled boulder-guts
of the man who searched and searched
for the elusive sign—
    the rabbit-legged cloud,
    the shape of the snake—
his dream a long migration
over red, red sand
beneath the low acacia trees
his guts bursting at last—
a swift canyon of despair,
a rocky tumble into dream time.

To remember is the same
as to dream, the old guide says—
to be in that place
which is not here,
cannot be seen or touched,
yesterday as invisible,
as remote as last night's stars,
the past a flicker
on the same screen as sleep.

I could tell another legend:
there is a woman I know
who dreamed three love affairs:
    a November lake
    a runner in sand
    whales diving in a northern sea.

She too is searching.
What she has not learned
are the facts of history—
that the migration of love
cannot enter another's dreaming time,
cannot always explain
those tracks on the face
of the old, old moon,
the meaning of boulders.

Wellington

for Varvara

This July, this winter
of reversed perceptions,
we flew south into a storm so mean
the plane shuddered like a bumblebee
across the bay. Two were already dead
below us—the police launch
splitting like an oyster
when the storm slit its shell,
the road past Seatoun closed.

It was a week of closures:
the play we braved Chinatown
to see, the cable car, the dark
coming down like a fist.
At lunch on Lambton Quay,
I told you of the man I left,
my face coming clear
in the mirror again,
the eyes of insomnia
shut. That night
the phone rang an ending
in our hotel: your husband's voice
connected somewhere else.
This is a windy bit
I have to row, you said.
We closed the drapes
against the ripping sound.

Photographs: North Island

I. Lake Waikaremoana

The children of Tane
hid in these woods—
light-skinned, red-haired,
naked as their flutes—
or so the legend says.

I believe it.
Light is different here
deep in the bush.
Refracted on the polar ice,
it splinters on the lake,
makes a harlequin of shade.

I do not tell you this,
but bits of me elude the air,
dance behind the rimu trees.

II. Pirongia

Maidens seeking fernroot
took this path,
silver fronds brushing against them,
fingers of mist trailing their hair.
And some of them heard spectral flutes—
the koauau or putorino—
luring them up, up
to the summit of fog,
the mossy beds of giants
who were not men,
who could pipe away their wills,
enthrall them with music forever.

At the top of the trail
we find a goat skull stuck
in a small dead tree,
a clearing stripped of fern.
Those who slept with giants
never returned, you tell me.

We laugh, begin our descent
to the bellbird's song.
Then lichen on the trees,
clinging like hoarfrost.
Here and everywhere:
small, skeletal desires.

III. Rangitaiki River

Rapids, rocks,
water lacing the air.
In the photo, we've been pitched
to the bottom of the raft.
I will remember the quiet stretch:
the flight of the fan-tail
beside us. The wood pigeon
perched and at rest.

IV. Cape Reinga
      for Kate and Lin

This is the last
of the ends of the earth,
land's finger pointing straight
to the departure place, straight
to the old pohutakawa tree
where the *wairua* leaped—

stripped spirits of the dead—
when the seas collided
and bull-kelp surged aside,
and water was the last,
the most sacred entrance.

It is said the *wairua*
tied flax leaves in knots,
plaiting their long journey north,
rustled unseen through toi-toi
and bracken, the warriors in platoons
when the battle was lost, women
leaving nikau leaves, treeferns,
ghostly obsidian tokens.

We stand at the border
of force with force, sea
with sea, the blue Pacific
abutting the greener Tasman.
On the last slope
below the lighthouse drop,
we pose without fear
against the edge of the sky.
We are friends. We have crossed
what we needed to cross.
The flax is green, the air
untangled, the sunlight arrives
and arrives . . .

Photographs: South Island

for Avis, my niece

I. Otago Peninsula

Remember this
about that secret bay:

the paddock cliffs,
the hoof-wide trail, penguins
homing in the evening light,
their clown-shoe route
across the slanted sun . . .

And this: the one who stood
sentry on the rocks,
luring us away from nests,
from home, from lupines
flowing like the valley's veil,
to an absence of sound,
of speech, an absence of all
but the way we drew breath,
the penguin on the edge
of nothing but itself,
rocks remaining rocks,
the sea, the sea.

II. Franz Joseph Glacier: The Terminal Moraine

This is a place for the middle-aged—
the signposts marking year by year
the glacier's retreat, the past
a long scar of splintered rock.

And you, dear heart, are young,
your bandana more flagrant
than the Danger sign
as you climb up and up
to the avalanche zone.

What would I tell you
if I could call from this ridge?
Not: "Stay!" Not: "Be frightened!"
But that trees are reclaiming
this cicatrix of rock, lichen
softening the cuts, vines binding up.
From where I sit, waiting in rain,
nothing despairs here,
nothing denies.

III. St. Kilda Coast

Women on their own
wake like this, wind rocking
a beach motel, the rain chanting
alone, alone . . .
Our cameras packed,
we focus voices across the dark,
across the strangeness
of related lives, naming towns,
parents, the secrets we kept
from the family hearth, old
storms that now invade the room . . .

A tremor of nerves
I say of the wind,
a former lover's moan . . .

No, you say—a tympani.
The orchestra trips you took
too young. The vibraphone.

Another Journal: New Zealand, 1895

This is a history of spaces,
not wars, not farms
ripped like green transgressions from these hills.
This is about needles lost in floorboards
and griddles made from broken saws,
about the way
he felt for something in my skirts
on the voyage over, my father already dead,
my sister swept to sea
in an illness like a storm.

"This land
is ours," he wrote that winter
of berries, fern roots ("eat
what the Maoris eat"), green kea parrots,
their underwings already bled
with colors of the womb. I did the dutiful:
potatoes and parsnips, stones
for my own hearth when we moved
from the *whare,* the fern hut
whose shadows were my bridal lace.

His ledgers are on the shelf:
wages, crops, a visit from an Auckland judge,
the price of cemetery plots. I stitched
another story in a quilt: the shape
of tiny fish-mouths on my nipples
when the pain was done, the pleasured swirl
of the element we swam in; round "o's"
for the "ought" of an egg, for spaces
underground where steam vents forth,
where glowworms cast
their fishing nets; ovals
for the sounds of these new names:
Oamaru. Te Awamutu. Rotorua . . .

At sixty-eight I learned to write.

What does it mean
to make a mark on the ledger's page,
to tell as men tell, fixing forever
the color of uncertain skies?

Some pages I leave empty.
Some pages for the times I stood
at the kitchen window
or the bottom paddock pool,
not touching anything,
feeling myself a vacancy
not even clouds could fill.
Sometimes I wonder
what colors would explode
if I were to rise a little from the earth
and could push back the air,
could move myself into the space
between my body and the sky?

Waitomo: The River under the Earth

When we had descended far enough
I remembered it all:
    How it is dark
    when you enter the boat
    how the others are strangers
    how the ferryman is silent
    having warned in some upper passage
    that the current will be swift.

I said nothing
as he poled us through the water,
though some among us murmured,
some among us turned.
What good was there in speaking?
—Everyone I loved
was in another country,
everything I owned
was locked away and far.

I watched those we had left grow smaller,
black shapes on a black and weary shore.
This is Lethe, I said,
but I meant Styx. I meant Charon
and all those old stories,
all those crossings
that can never be recrossed.

When darkness was thicker than the water,
I remembered the rest.
I dropped the little I was holding,
turned my face upward as we had been told.
Glowworms clustered somewhere above us—
a newly constellated heaven
of blue and equal stars—
and long before the passage widened,
I knew the rhythm of the river,
long before the light came,
I was ready to float free.

from
*A Breeze Called the Fremantle
Doctor*
(1997)

Selections from

The Indian School

Pipestone, Minnesota, 1930–31

These schools should be conducted upon lines best adapted to the development of character, and the formation of habits of industrial thrift and moral responsibility, which will prepare the pupil for the active responsibilities of citizenship.

Rules for the Indian School Service, p. 3

Give the Indian a white man's chance. Educate him in the rudiments of our language, teach him to work. . . . It will exterminate the Indian but develop a man.

Commissioner William A. Jones, 1903

Preface

I began to search for my mother when she had almost disappeared. "Here, you take these," she said, thrusting a box of jumbled scrapbooks and photo albums at me the summer my father's stroke convinced her to move from the farmhouse to an apartment near his nursing home. I was back in Minnesota to help her get organized, to get rid of the effluvium of eighty years so that my siblings would have an easier time with the actual move. In this mission, I failed entirely. She would throw away nothing. She would take a dusty piece of driftwood stuck with plastic flowers from a cupboard shelf, muse about which of her friends might have made it, and then put it back while I held a garbage bag open and empty.

Now and then she would offer me things: a mildewed picnic basket, a cookie jar missing its lid. Putting them in my car seemed the only way to get rid of anything, and I'm enough of a family historian to want the photos and scrapbooks preserved. But I didn't make much of them; I glanced through and put them in my attic when I got home. Meanwhile, things worsened. My mother hated the apartment, hated living alone, became so erratic mentally that we weren't surprised by the diagnosis we feared: Alzheimer's, advancing its inexorable march through her brain cells. Now the farm had to be sold to pay for both their care, and from the depths of a closet emerged a box of letters I never knew existed—a lot of letters, three years worth of weekly data and dreaming between a young couple deterred from marriage by the Great Depression, a young couple who weren't my parents yet. "She said she wants you to have them," my brother said, presenting me with the carton. "I think she hopes you'll write something."

I wasn't thrilled by the implied assignment. My mother's usual response to my writing had been to say, "Well, that's very nice, honey," and then to tell me everything about the piece that was factually wrong. My mother was usually sure of what was right. She was the most educated woman in our farm community, and in my young eyes, the most powerful. She knew everything: the recipe for lye soap, how to make bound buttonholes, which magazines were wholesome enough for children to read, and why it was silly to fear public speaking. She was the neighborhood arbiter, adviser, organist, barber, and reference desk, and at times I resented it. At times I stayed in my room with pencil and paper and created worlds she couldn't critique.

Now this most competent of women had no power at all, and I was having trouble dealing with that. While she forgot where I lived and what I did, I spent the long evenings of a summer reading letters by a young woman who was surprisingly tentative, dependent on her father's advice, giddy with her first teaching success. As she forgot my name and how to tie her shoes, I poured over scrapbooks and albums, urgent to construct a woman who would not be my mother for a dozen years.

I say "construct" deliberately. Even letters are ruled by the prevailing discourse of the time, and these were bulky with slang and chitchat about mutual friends, coy about admitting love, nearly silent about major events: their engagement, her father's death. The scraps and fragments I found most intriguing were those from the year she taught at the Pipestone Indian Training School, perhaps because she'd seemed so proud of that experience, perhaps because in later years she kept reminding me that she could have been a career woman too.

I made a trip to Pipestone the next summer. I walked the trail through the quarry to Winniwissa Falls, brought back samples of the flesh-red stone used for centuries of peace pipes, and waded through the archives of the historical museum. I didn't find my mother anywhere at all, but I realized I really didn't need to find her. We select our memories, consciously or not. We weave the tales that explain to ourselves our lives. My mother knew I was a creature given to invention when she consigned the letters to my keeping. At some level, she must also have known I'd use those hints and scraps to construct the woman and the tale I most needed to hear.

1. Home Economics

I who said I would never teach
am learning now, white
girl caught in the stampede
of 1930, Pa's hatchery gone,
the gristmill faltering,
my fair-skinned love
wheeling amid the weaning calves,
the cows dried up, oats
still in shocks no one will buy,
a five-acre bog of potatoes.

The baby chicks,
his last nest-egg hope,
sucked beneath the floor-boards—
seventeen in one night,
twenty-four the next,
a single rat wrapping its tail
round both our dreams.

And I here,
an endless plain away, white
in my apron and cap,
my baking powder, flour bins,
my recipes for shortbread,
dumplings, thrift. I,
for ninety dollars a month,
stumble into the brown distrust
of eyes that buy nothing,
give nothing away.

2. Civilization

Miss Perry says I should not decorate
with tepees, feathered hoops, the strange bent cross
girls doodle in the flour on their kneading boards.
(Miss Perry, nearly forty, is my cottage mate.)

Miss Perry says these kids don't need a nudge—
they go "back to the blanket" anyway
—to shacks and dogs and filthy pagan ways.
Miss Perry has been westward to Pine Ridge.

The rules come to us from Washington:
no blankets, no beads, no speaking in Sioux,
no hair worn long, no going home till June.
Miss Perry is sorry for the little ones.

We're here to show them the way, she says,
to make decent, Christian, tidy homes.
Miss Perry has a bible in her room.
I keep my rosary right beside the bed.

6. Influenza

Last night in the infirmary,
I watched the prairie thicken,
darkness viscous as the syrup
I dispensed for coughs. The nurse,
burning with a fever of her own,
left me only this instruction:
keep them quieted down.

Nine girls on first floor,
seven boys above, their breaths
a dozen tones of long-grass
weaving in a prairie wind.

How was I to recognize delirium—
a sudden terror moving through the beds,
Hector Esau jolting up,
crying out in Sioux?

"Speak English, Hector," I told him.
"It's a nightmare, a fever-dream.
Wake up!" But for all the good it did,
I might have been a milkweed fluff,
a peeping fledgling in the prairie's hum.

The current ran down both the rows.
"He sees somebody,"
Jimmy Tall Horse said,
"He sees in the window. This is bad."

"This is second floor," I said,
"there's nothing outside but night."
"Maybe it's his brother," Jimmy said.
"His brother died last year. Right here.
At night. Maybe they released his soul . . ."

"Maybe *who* released his soul?" I said,
but silence fell like a linen pall
across their eyes. "He couldn't go home,
he couldn't get real medicine . . ."
the smallest of them said,
and that was all.

I don't know who slept last night,
and who lay still, young rabbits
freezing to elude a hawk.
I prowled the rows of beds,
stalked the dark panes
for all I've heard:

witches and medicine-men,
raiders dead and alive,
sweat lodge and worshipped sun,
mumbo jumbo and all that's vile.

Morning came on schedule,
and none of my patients died.
But why was my report so brief:
     one girl's fever broke,
     one boy had dreams.

And did I imagine
those whispers through the night,
like a clear and distant bell:
     Don't tell, Miss B.
     Don't tell. Don't tell.

10. Pipestone

Before they could approach
the quarry ledge,
they smoked kinnikinic—
tobacco, red willow bark,
a seasoning of prairie herbs.
They bathed in Winniwissa's stream,
left women in the camp, paused
at Wa-root-ka's sacred rocks,
to leave their sacrifice.

If, at daybreak, a totem appeared
scratched somewhere in the stone,
they were worthy to point
heavenward the lighted pipe,
point all four corners of the universe,
point downward to earth,
begging permission
to break her skin,
to find in her veins
this sacred stone.

Indian Joe in his quarry hut
told me this. He carves
paperweights, arrowheads,
the little pipe I'm sending you.

Pipestone is part of our flesh,
he said, *red men a part of this stone.*

Then, why do you sell it? I said,
looking off toward the quarry shelf.
This is a place of peace, he said,
war clubs are buried, angers gone.

The seventh direction is self,
he said. *When you white men pray,*
does it come from breath—
does it come from bone?

14. Spheres

I was my father's oldest,
his right-hand girl, his "hired man,"
preening as we harnessed the Clydesdales,
the Belgian roans, a double team
for the four-gang plow I alone
was old enough to manage.

                    That spring,
when his peacocks were molting,
when I tucked an iridescent eye
into each brass bridle ring
and plowed the corner turns
precise as quilted squares,
I measured time by the gold
of his pocket watch, dreaming
as it slipped its chain, planted itself
somewhere in the back quarter section.

I knew that time does not reverse itself,
that pride precedes an object's fall,
that the losses we sow
we must also reap, but my father
who knew nothing of circles
in Indian lore, said only,
"Maybe it will sprout,"
reached, and ruffled my hair.

> Imagine a gold seed ticking.
> Imagine slender stalks like minute hands.
> Imagine each blossom giving us back
> some piece of the past that we've used up.

Imagine life
as a circle of days, a ring of years,
a bright and burnished hoop
that brings us back
to each of our beginnings.

18. Midnight

My first taste of midnight
was the time I helped with lambing,
the year that I was twelve.
I did not know then
that any female opening
was made so wide, so wet,
so full of slime and slippery coatings,
slick as stock-tank algae
afloat in summer shade.

When it was over,
I went to stand at the barn's half-door,
the moon a silver sickle,
the stars just out of reach.
Pa came to stand beside me
but we did not speak.

The prairie was a band of blackness,
the wind a lowing sound. I knew,
for him, that *longing* meant the old,
the other country; for me, new space
to enter in. But both of us
were standing at love's margin,
at the vast ache of a treeless plain
where nothing calls and nothing moves
except the lower layers of your skin.

21. Assembly: The Man from Antarctica

As the sun went down for the last time, the darkness closed in and the aurora jerked into fantastic patterns across the sky.
— Admiral Richard Byrd

Imagine months of night,
he says; imagine cold so brisk
it would break your whiskers off.
Imagine life as moles
tunnelling from hut to hut
beneath a sky of snow.

Some men had visions, he says:
sun sparking the snow like flint,
frozen lakes aflame, infernos
of ice, light igniting
at the back of the eye.

Some ate blubber, he says;
some ate dog. Some ate nothing,
and staggered whirling
through dervishes of snow.

Why do men do this?
Why fast, why freeze,
why sweat as the Dakota do
in a stinking lodge?
Is there another world this side of death
where the "great mysterious"
truly can be known?

Imagine a compass pointing
straight up to the sky.
Imagine a day of shadowless sun.

Imagine a crevasse so deep
that as you fall
rainbows shatter beside you.

Imagine a magnet pulling.
Imagine your own true north.

26. Release

Hector, when his brother died,
slashed both his arms, sliced
in half his blankets and his sheets,
gave away the pipestone bits
he'd been allowed to keep.

No suicide attempt, Miss Perry says;
some old and pagan custom
about the way to grieve.

"Did they keep his soul"?
I ask, "—the brother's soul?"

"Oh, that," Miss Perry laughs.
"The government—the B.I.A.—
banned that nonsense
forty years ago—ordered
the Sioux on a certain day
to release all souls they kept."

But who could check
if they did or not?—and where
do freed souls go?

Did they swirl like genies
from the tepee's center hole?
Did they rush long and low
scaring the prairie grass
like bobcats gaining speed?

To keep a soul within a house
would be to let all earthly things
give way. To fast and weep,
and sleep upon a bed
of sacred sage, the mind
a sheet stretched out
to capture any dreams.

To keep a soul
would be a lover's act,
a wild flower pressed
at dawn each day, a lock
of hair in a well-worn book,
a horizon so clean and bare
you'd sense a presence there at once,
no matter how empty it seemed.

32. Calumet

White Buffalo Woman,
she who walked out of mystery
into a Lakota camp,
had a red pipe in her bundle.

> *The bowl of red stone is Mother Earth*
> *The carved calf is the four-legs who live upon her*
> *The stem is the wood of all that grows*
> *The feathers of all that soar*
> *Every dawn is a holy event*
> *Every step on our Mother a prayer*
> *With Wakan Tanka I am walking . . .*

What is that, I ask Mindy—*Wakan Tanka?*

The Great Mysterious, she says,
breath you can see, breath that creates,
life breath of the universe.
Do you believe me?

I believe in the Catholic God, I say:
Father, Son and Holy Ghost.

I hear myself say it: *Holy*

Ghost.

Selections from

A Breeze Called the Fremantle Doctor

Fremantle, Western Australia, 1864–1993

. . . a pleasant coolness in the heat,
solace in the midst of woe . . .

> Sequence for Pentecost
> Stephen Langton, 1228

Preface

I went to Western Australia in 1993 because I couldn't think of a good reason not to go. I had the requisite experience to work with university students in a foreign setting, and a change of climate might be good for a crippling headache syndrome brought on by the approach of menopause. So when I was asked to go to a new study-abroad program in Fremantle with twenty-five Notre Dame students, I said yes, but with misgivings. The Perth/Fremantle area stands in isolation on the western edge of the map, a dot in a vast emptiness, and I didn't know if I could handle the heat.

Nighttimes weren't too bad. The ocean breeze the Aussies call "the doctor" did, as advertised, come in most afternoons or evenings to cool things off. My office and classroom were air-conditioned; but weekends were a problem: my top-floor flat was scorching at midday. After a few weekends of matinees, long lunches, and riding the air-cooled commuter train to Perth and back, I discovered an old limestone building with an almost monastic inner courtyard. There, in deep shade, I could listen to folk singers and poetry readings, could sip fruit drinks from the little snack shop and browse the indoor exhibits. I came to think of Fremantle's Art Centre and Museum as a place of refuge, refreshment, solace, not just from heat, but from the inevitable loneness of a stranger in a strange, though beautiful, land. The word "asylum" kept coming to my mind.

That word proved to be apt. When I got around to reading the Centre's brochure, I discovered that it was built in 1864 as the Fremantle Asylum for "Lunatics." Convict labor quarried the stone, native jarrah wood framed the rooms, and into them came men and women for whom there were no trains and electric fans, for whom the only way of coping with harsh and unforgiving terrain was to leave it, to let the mind slip its moorings even as the body remained. A new friend, Phillipa Ryan, told me that a woman in her family tree had been committed there after the birth of her last child. Perhaps it was only postpartum depression, Phillipa said, but according to family legend, the woman lived for years and years and never left the limestone walls.

That woman began to follow me. Her footsteps echoed as I moved from room to room in the Centre, as my heels rang on the old jarrah stairs. Though I flourished in Fremantle's unpolluted light, and became bold enough to make solo expeditions into the sunburnt plains beyond the escarpment, I always traveled with a sense of earlier travelers, of women who thrust themselves—or were thrust by their lives—into barely discovered countries of place, or position, or mind. Theirs were the lives I wanted to investigate. Theirs were the stories I wanted to tell.

Asylum 1883–1916: Margaret

Whether I was truly in Australia at all,
or whether in the body, or out of the body—
I cannot tell; but I have had bad dreams.

—John Mitchel

Increase in population brings with it an increase in lunacy.

—Surgeon Superintendent Barnett, 1886

1. Margaret: Commitment

I did not try to kill the baby.
No matter what he said,
no matter what they wrote
in that leather-bound book,
that record of wildness,
its pages restrained
like the lunatics
whose names went down
spider after inky spider,
scrambling to escape the page.

I know what they wrote.
I know what my husband told them,
standing there wringing his hat
like a pullet's neck.
"Can we eat that?" I said.
"Can we eat that like the chickens
that were going to scratch, scratch
in the bloody red dirt and make us
a blooming fortune?"

"She says things that don't make sense,"
he said. "Sometimes she don't talk at all.
It's too much for me," he said,
"too much for all the little ones,
for Gemma, first of the lot
and her just after turning twelve."

Let him say what he wants;
I did not leave the baby to die.
I left it to live, live
but somewhere else,
to become a goanna,
changing colors as it moves,
to become a quick lizard
becoming one with the sand.

2. Margaret: Confinement

They have made us into chickens
penned in the glare of an afternoon,
our white dresses smoothed by hands
that roam and roam
with nowhere to perch,
our combs of red sorrow
our wattles of rage
clipped, clipped
like wings, like the shadow
we cannot escape
in this cloister of a courtyard.

"You'll be peaceful here,"
he said, but that's a laugh.
What kind of peace
can limestone give
when every step rattles
old bones of jarrah wood,
and there's nothing in your arms
but the ghost of a baby
you did not kill,
and it lived, lived,
though nothing lives here
but the ghosts of chickens,
chooks they say,
cackle, cackle, all day long,
the face you had
gone to nothing now,
pale as limestone
splattered with sun,
and asylum is a bit of shade,
a bit of green, a sail

in the purple river of sunset,
the green river of blood
that courses through
the back of hands that will not,
will not be still.

3. Margaret: Lessons

They did it in Cornwall.
I know this for truth:
put the newborn babe
on the new tilled earth,
on nights of no or little moon.
I suppose it cried; I suppose
it was cold, but exposure
was brief, and better to know
which direction earth pulls,
how little space abides
between the waters of the womb
and the land's soggy maw.

I put mine in a cave of rock,
red-rimmed, boulder strewn.
I planned to nurse it
evenings, mornings, noons,
to let it try to affix itself,
as I can never be affixed
to a soil not soil, but sand.

I wanted to harden it,
as soap must harden
to be more than fat and lye,
to season it
as new pots are taught
to be separate from food.
I would have watched
its color change
with each new sky;
I would have told it
that in empty land
no loneliness
is deeper than a mother's.

4. Margaret: Wind

All the chooks work in the laundry shed
where the cauldron heats, and the lye—
the lie—that we cleanse men's clothes
comes clean when we cannot cleanse
our own souls, our own bodies
of the hot spume men leave in us,
as the cattle leave dust—not steaming
cowpats here, but turds, dry turds
that give birth to flies that stick
to eyes, to nose, till every bit of excrement,
even the childrens' left behind a bush,
is alive, alive, moving and creeping forward,
closer to sand, to dust, to which
we are destined to return,

and returning once from Geraldton,
we stopped on a shore of such
white sand I thought I saw snow
there, in the heat, in the dryness,
in the sand around the Pinnacles,
those spires of rock,
so late in the moon
I thought they were standing stones,
runes the Old Ones erected,
but they told me no, no,
the blackfellas never erected these
—only wind and waves and thousands
of years—or Kangaroo-man and
Wallaby-man in the darkness
of the Dreamtime,

but *all* here is dream, a fever of time
that never was, a view of hell
in an ice-blue sea, and if only
I did not have to catch
so many little souls
and turn them into bodies, as I
have done seven times, though two
are dead, and this one, this one
I planned to keep pale, to keep
from leathering, as we used to keep
cream in the springhouse so it was
cool, cool

as a body can be, but I
do not have a body,
I have melted from heat, from
the colors of childbirth
all run together, and I

I have become a wind.

5. Margaret: Jackeroo

I was not always made of air.
In Devon, I was an earthly lass,
but earth shifted, and I
had to cross when my mother crossed—
she to her just reward, I to Wooloona,
Aunt Ada and a cooking shack,
on sheep land west of Melbourne.

I met my husband in the evening shade—
I watering the little pippin trees
come from Cornwall
with their promise of fruit,
he, a green hand but older,
smelling of sheep-dip, the oil
of fleeces he could not yet shear.
I thought that we were suited—
I, the orphan, and he, the jackeroo—
were new, fresh, green
as the countries we left behind,
eager as border collies.

Eagerness is not enough,
and the land back-of-beyond
is always there tempting.
We moved as labor to a hill farm,
a cattle station, a godforsaken
chunk of dirt where he
attempted raising pigs. Then
he heard of the goldfields,
then of free land in the far,
far west.

Each move
I carried another child. Each move
I tried to leave behind regret.

6. Margaret: Conception

Blackfella women "catch" their babies
from the Dreamtime beasts, snag
a wallaby-spirit in wallaby land,
a honey-bee child in a space that's sweet.

Black Maisie told me this,
working in the dairy shed, days
she didn't have the urge
to go walkabout, to dig turtle eggs,
to sneak my soap down to the billabong
and make bubbles for her kangaroo boy,
her goanna girl, sudsing up
the little our cattle had to drink.

"Babies come from men," I told her,
"from the brine they leave inside."

"You funny missus," Maisie said.
"Men in you *all* time.
Bad time come—no baby.
Food no good—no baby.
Baby, him suck—no new baby.
Spirit angry—no baby to catch."

Then why did I catch so many? And worse:
why did I love them each? Why take
to my breast bodies slippery from birth
and feel myself plunge into warmth
so vast, an ocean so deep
I thought I could never feel rain,
never know again the presence
of unrelenting heat?

What did that lightness drain from me?
How does a desert continue to bloom?

7. Margaret: Cave

When Chester died in Victoria,
my first and green-eyed boy,
I buried him next to Aunt Ada's cross
on a wee and windy hill.
When Nellie blazed here,
fever shooting through her like a star,
there was scarce enough wood
for the little box, no flower
but the bottle-brush, no place
on the vast escarpment
for her to nestle in.

I have never nestled. Five months gone
with my seventh one, I made
my own shade, began to roam
toward Nellie's grave, toward dusk,
toward a little snuggery of acacia bush
fronting a boulder-spill—giant loaves
lurched from a red-orange soil,
pumpkins dropped from a cosmic cart.

One eve, Black Maisie stood
in the shadow of the boulders.
"Woman place. Secret," she said,
pointing through the acacia bush.
"Much dreaming. Much strong. Old."
She looked at my belly, swollen
already with this year's catch.
"Girl baby," she said, "Honey bee,"
and she held the branches
as I ducked behind her, stood in eerie light
beneath an overhang of presences
faded but aglow: large, mouthless heads,
haloes of ochre rays, stick-women
with winnowing bowls, handprints
stenciled by a spray of white.

I reasoned how this should go:
I would bring indigo or ink,
trace the baby's fingers,
her little palm, know
she could belong to this place,
her breath part of the dreaming,
her hands part of the stone.

8. Margaret: Violation

I told him
I felt peaceful within the rock;
I contained an inner breeze.
I told him women's blood
disappears, month by month,
red earth by earth, and we
must draw our palm-prints
onto sacred stone to stay. I told him
the child was safe, the deed
was done, but he dragged me
from the house, forced me
to straddle the horse
ahead of him.

I told him
the cave was women-space,
forbidden, it's power bad
for men, but he slapped me
into the acacia bush, grabbed
the child, and with a stone
raked across the palm-print,
slashed the women with winnowing bowls,
ground out the auras of yellow light,
the faces watchful and old.

I told him
I was no longer his wife.
I told him he had killed the baby's soul.
I told him I would walk not ride,
and I did not go home.

9. Margaret: Corroboree

And then I descended into darkness.
I became black, and I walked
beyond myself into a space
back of the billabong
where native fires burned
and the blackfellas painted
not stone but self
in great swaths of white—
white dots big as smallpox, white
diamonds, white squares. Aprons
of eucalypt covered their privates,
ruffs of gum leaves shook
their ankles into storm.

Women beat time on possum skins;
men clacked sticks seared in flame.
A didgeridoo hollowed the air
and singing carved the night.
I do not know what cause
they had to celebrate, why
young men seemed to split
themselves, their legs quivering
closer and closer to the ground,
their bodies a trunk, a tree
in which the smallest birds
could come to rest.

I split too, and when
the dancing was done,
I pulled the dawn around me;
I became a dream
as I have since become the wind.

10. Margaret, 1916:
The Fremantle Residence for Poor Ladies

I am not a lunatic now.
Thirty years onward,
I have been renamed,
reclassified, left here
as indigent, aged,
harmless even to the self,
the other lunatics gone,
packed and shipped
to a new coop up in Claremont.

I do not really need a name.
I ride easy in the light
of morning, afternoon, schooled
to need nothing and therefore
be rich. From the garden
I see ships in the harbor; I hear
a parrot above me, its cry
counting the skies: *eighty-six,
eighty-six, eighty-six.*

I no longer count what happens,
and I do not know
where my children live.
Some nights before sleep,
the velvet of small bodies
lies next to mine,
but to remember is to dream,
and to dream is to gather

the thinnest threads that memory spins
and twine them into songs
to map the road you'll travel by.
And, to enter the *Dreaming,*
as Maisie well knew,
is to sing outside of time,
to dream outside of sleep,
to let the spirit know at last the truth:

there is no difference
between the body and the breeze.

Asylum 1993: Sonia

I love a sunburnt country . . . a willful, lavish land . . .
                    —Dorothea MacKellar

When you set out for Ithaka
Pray that your road's a long one . . .
                    —C.P. Cavafy